16LIVES
CON COLBERT

The 16LIVES Series

JAMES CONNOLLY Lorcan Collins

MICHAEL MALLIN Brian Hughes

JOSEPH PLUNKETT Honor O Brolchain

EDWARD DALY Helen Litton

SEÁN HEUSTON John Gibney

ROGER CASEMENT Angus Mitchell

SEÁN MACDIARMADA Brian Feeney

THOMAS CLARKE Helen Litton

ÉAMONN CEANNT Mary Gallagher

THOMAS MACDONAGH Shane Kenna

WILLIE PEARSE Roisín Ní Ghairbhí

CON COLBERT John O'Callaghan

JOHN MACBRIDE Donal Fallon

MICHAEL O'HANRAHAN Conor Kostick

THOMAS KENT Meda Ryan

PATRICK PEARSE Ruán O'Donnell

JOHN O'CALLAGHAN – AUTHOR OF 16LIVES: CON COLBERT

Dr John O'Callaghan lectures in St Angela's College, Sligo. His
research focuses on twentieth-century Ireland and processes
of imperialism and nationalism, as well as sports history
and commemoration. His publications include: *Teaching Irish
Independence: History in Irish Schools, 1922–72* (2009); *Revolutionary
Limerick – The Republican Campaign for Independence, 1913–21*
(2010); *The Battle for Kilmallock* (2011); *Subversive Voices: Narratives of the
Occluded Irish Diaspora* (2012); and *Plassey's Gaels: GAA in the* University of
Limerick (2013).

LORCAN COLLINS – SERIES EDITOR

Lorcan Collins was born and raised in Dublin. A lifelong interest
in Irish history led to the foundation of his hugely-popular 1916
Walking Tour in 1996. He co-authored *The Easter Rising: A Guide
to Dublin in 1916* (O'Brien Press, 2000) with Conor Kostick. His
biography of James Connolly was published in the *16 Lives* series
in 2012. He is also a regular contributor to radio, television and historical
journals. *16 Lives* is Lorcan's concept and he is co-editor of the series.

DR RUÁN O'DONNELL – SERIES EDITOR

Dr Ruán O'Donnell is a senior lecturer at the University of Limerick.
A graduate of University College Dublin and the Australian
National University, O'Donnell has published extensively on Irish
Republicanism. Titles include *Robert Emmet and the Rising of 1803,
The Impact of 1916* (editor), *Special Category, The IRA in English prisons
1968–1978* and *The O'Brien Pocket History of the Irish Famine*. He is a director
of the Irish Manuscript Commission and a frequent contributor to the national
and international media on the subject of Irish revolutionary history.

16LIVES
CON COLBERT

John O'Callaghan

**Waterford City and County
Libraries**

THE O'BRIEN PRESS
DUBLIN

First published 2015 by
The O'Brien Press Ltd,
12 Terenure Road East, Rathgar,
Dublin 6, Ireland.
Tel: +353 1 4923333; Fax: +353 1 4922777
E-mail: books@obrien.ie.
Website: www.obrien.ie

ISBN: 978-1-84717-334-8
Text © copyright John O'Callaghan 2015
Copyright for typesetting, layout, editing, design
© The O'Brien Press Ltd
Series concept: Lorcan Collins

8 7 6 5 4 3 2 1
18 17 16 15

All quotations, in English and Irish, have been reproduced with original spelling and punctuation.

Printed and bound by CPI Group (UK) Ltd, Croydon, CR0 4YY
The paper used in this book is produced using pulp from managed forests.

PICTURE CREDITS

The author and publisher wish to thank the following for permission to use photographs
and illustrative material:
Picture Section 1: Allen Library p.1, p.2 (both), p.4 (bottom); Maeve O'Leary p.3 (both);
Des Long p.6 (top); National Library of Ireland p.6 (bottom); Des Long p.7 (top);
Kilmainham Gaol p.7 (bottom); Bureau of Military History p.8.
Picture Section 2: RTÉ p.2 (top); National Museum p.2 (bottom), p.6 (top); Kilmainham
Gaol p.3; Mick O'Farrell p.4 (middle); Fusiliers Museum of Northumberland p.5 (top);
Pádraig Ó Ruairc p.5 (bottom), p.7; Irish Capuchin Provincial Archives p.6 (bottom); Ray
Bateson p.8.

DEDICATION

I gcuimhne ar John O'Callaghan – m'athair agus mo chara.

ACKNOWLEDGEMENTS

Almost a century after his death, this is the first full-scale biography of Con Colbert. There is no guarantee of another. So, rather than confining his voice to footnotes or appendices, Colbert's personal letters and poetry are placed front and centre in the text beside the narrative of his actions. Thanks to the 16 Lives series co-editors, Ruán O'Donnell, who invited me to write this book, and Lorcan Collins, for his enthusiastic support throughout. The staff of a variety of archival institutions were most obliging: the Allen Library, the Irish Capuchin Provincial Archives, the Fusiliers Museum of Northumberland, Kilmainham Gaol, Limerick City Library, the Military Archives of Ireland, the National Archives of Ireland, the National Archives of the United Kingdom, the National Library of Ireland, the National Museum of Ireland, the Pearse Museum, and University of Limerick Library Special Collections. A host of individuals were generous with their knowledge and their time: Ray Bateson, Niall Bergin, Noelle Cawley, Finbarr Connolly, Patricia Conway, Liam Clarke, Con Colbert, John Colbert, Brian Crowley, Liam Doherty, Úna Gonley, Simone Hickey, Brian Hughes, Lar Joye, Commandant Pádraig Kennedy, Rosemary King, Jim Langton, Corporal Andrew Lawlor, John Logan, Des Long, Patrick Mannix, Séamus McAlwee, James McDonald, Eamon Murphy, Sarah Nolan, Pádraig Óg Ó Ruairc, Mick O'Farrell, Maeve O'Leary, Seosamh Mac Muirí, Elaine Sisson, and Tom Toomey. Mairéad agus Seán Óg, is aoibhinn liom sibh.

16LIVES Timeline

1845–51. The Great Hunger in Ireland. One million people die and over the next decades millions more emigrate.

1858, March 17. The Irish Republican Brotherhood, or Fenians, are formed with the express intention of overthrowing British rule in Ireland by whatever means necessary.

1867, February and March. Fenian Uprising.

1870, May. Home Rule movement founded by Isaac Butt, who had previously campaigned for amnesty for Fenian prisoners.

1879–81. The Land War. Violent agrarian agitation against English landlords.

1884, November 1. The Gaelic Athletic Association founded – immediately infiltrated by the Irish Republican Brotherhood (IRB).

1893, July 31. Gaelic League founded by Douglas Hyde and Eoin MacNeill. The *Gaelic Revival*, a period of Irish Nationalism, pride in the language, history, culture and sport.

1900, September. *Cumann na nGaedheal* (Irish Council) founded by Arthur Griffith.

1905–07. *Cumann na nGaedheal*, the Dungannon Clubs and the National Council are amalgamated to form *Sinn Féin* (We Ourselves).

1909, August. Countess Markievicz and Bulmer Hobson organise nationalist youths into *Na Fianna Éireann* (Warriors of Ireland) a kind of boy scout brigade.

1912, April. Asquith introduces the Third Home Rule Bill to the British Parliament. Passed by the Commons and rejected by the Lords, the Bill would have to become law due to the Parliament Act. Home Rule expected to be introduced for Ireland by autumn 1914.

1913, January. Sir Edward Carson and James Craig set up Ulster Volunteer Force (UVF) with the intention of defending Ulster against Home Rule.

1913. Jim Larkin, founder of the Irish Transport and General Workers' Union (ITGWU) calls for a workers' strike for better pay and conditions.

1913, August 31. Jim Larkin speaks at a banned rally on Sackville (O'Connell) Street; Bloody Sunday.

1913, November 23. James Connolly, Jack White and Jim Larkin establish the Irish Citizen Army (ICA) in order to protect strikers.

1913, November 25. The Irish Volunteers founded in Dublin to 'secure the rights and liberties common to all the people of Ireland'.

1914, March 20. Resignations of British officers force British government not to use British army to enforce Home Rule, an event known as the 'Curragh Mutiny'.

1914, April 2. In Dublin, Agnes O'Farrelly, Mary MacSwiney, Countess Markievicz and others establish Cumann na mBan as a women's volunteer force dedicated to establishing Irish freedom and assisting the Irish Volunteers.

1914, April 24. A shipment of 35,000 rifles and five million rounds of ammunition is landed at Larne for the UVF.

1914, July 26. Irish Volunteers unload a shipment of 900 rifles and 45,000 rounds of ammunition shipped from Germany aboard Erskine Childers' yacht, the *Asgard*. British troops fire on crowd on Bachelors Walk, Dublin. Three citizens are killed.

1914, August 4. Britain declares war on Germany. Home Rule for Ireland shelved for the duration of the First World War.

1914, September 9. Meeting held at Gaelic League headquarters between IRB and other extreme republicans. Initial decision made to stage an uprising while Britain is at war.

1914, September. 170,000 leave the Volunteers and form the National Volunteers or Redmondites. Only 11,000 remain as the Irish Volunteers under Eóin MacNeill.

1915, May–September. Military Council of the IRB is formed.

1915, August 1. Pearse gives fiery oration at the funeral of Jeremiah O'Donovan Rossa.

1916, January 19–22. James Connolly joins the IRB Military Council, thus ensuring that the ICA shall be involved in the Rising. Rising date confirmed for Easter.

1916, April 20, 4.15pm. *The Aud* arrives at Tralee Bay, laden with 20,000 German rifles for the Rising. Captain Karl Spindler waits in vain for a signal from shore.

1916, April 21, 2.15am. Roger Casement and his two companions go ashore from U-19 and land on Banna Strand. Casement is arrested at McKenna's Fort.

6.30pm. *The Aud* is captured by the British navy and forced to sail towards Cork Harbour.

22 April, 9.30am. *The Aud* is scuttled by her captain off Daunt's Rock.

10pm. Eóin MacNeill as chief-of-staff of the Irish Volunteers issues the countermanding order in Dublin to try to stop the Rising.

1916, April 23, 9am, Easter Sunday. The Military Council meets to discuss the situation, considering MacNeill has placed an advertisement in a Sunday newspaper halting all Volunteer operations. The Rising is put on hold for twenty-four hours. Hundreds of copies of *The Proclamation of the Republic* are printed in Liberty Hall.

1916, April 24, 12 noon, Easter Monday. The Rising begins in Dublin.

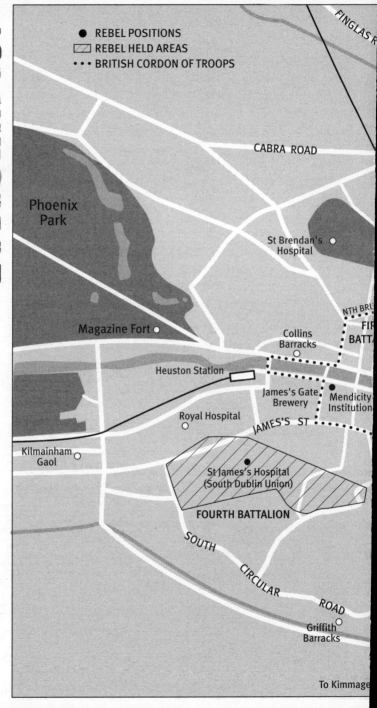

16 LIVES MAP

- ● REBEL POSITIONS
- ▨ REBEL HELD AREAS
- ••• BRITISH CORDON OF TROOPS

FINGLAS R

CABRA ROAD

Phoenix Park

St Brendan's Hospital

Magazine Fort ○

NTH BRU

FIR BATTA

Collins Barracks ○

Heuston Station

James's Gate Brewery

Mendicity Institution

Royal Hospital ○

JAMES'S ST

Kilmainham Gaol ○

St James's Hospital (South Dublin Union)

FOURTH BATTALION

SOUTH

CIRCULAR

ROAD

Griffith Barracks ○

To Kimmage

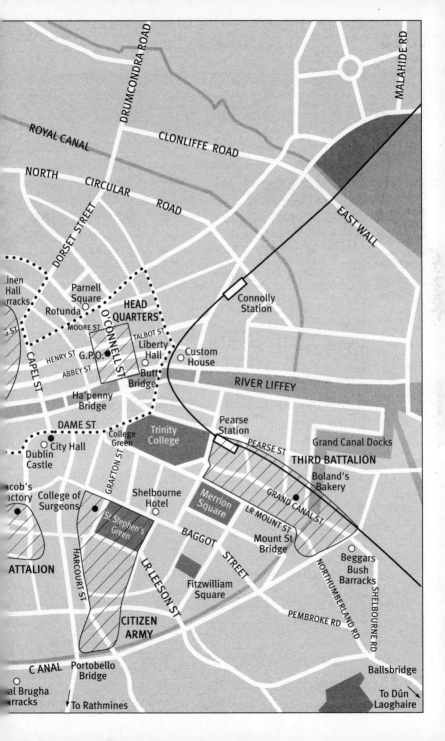

16LIVES – Series Introduction

This book is part of a series called *16 LIVES*, conceived with the objective of recording for posterity the lives of the sixteen men who were executed after the 1916 Easter Rising. Who were these people and what drove them to commit themselves to violent revolution?

The rank and file as well as the leadership were all from diverse backgrounds. Some were privileged and some had no material wealth. Some were highly educated writers, poets or teachers and others had little formal schooling. Their common desire, to set Ireland on the road to national freedom, united them under the one banner of the army of the Irish Republic. They occupied key buildings in Dublin and around Ireland for one week before they were forced to surrender. The leaders were singled out for harsh treatment and all sixteen men were executed for their role in the Rising.

Meticulously researched yet written in an accessible fashion, the *16 LIVES* biographies can be read as individual volumes but together they make a highly collectible series.

Lorcan Collins & Dr Ruán O'Donnell,
16 Lives *Series Editors*

CONTENTS

Introduction   15

Chapter 1: Home Life and Formative Influences   31

Chapter 2: Cultural Nationalist   45

Chapter 3: Na Fianna Éireann   67

Chapter 4: The Volunteers   96

Chapter 5: The Rising   131

Chapter 6: Court Martial and Execution   191

Chapter 7: Conclusion   225

Bibliography   232

Notes   236

Index   252

Introduction

In Newcastlewest in County Limerick, close to where Con Colbert was born and spent his childhood, a memorial to republican martyrs was erected in 1955. A catalogue informs visitors that Colbert fought in the General Post Office (GPO) during the 1916 Easter Rising, and that he was executed on 7 May. Neither part of this statement is factual. He was elsewhere in Dublin city centre – first in Watkins' brewery on Ardee Street and then in Jameson's distillery on Marrowbone Lane. He was executed on 8 May. Such inaccuracies might seem harmless in themselves – and this first instance merely reflects the centrality of the GPO to how the Rising is remembered – but they are indicative of the manner in which man and myth can become one.

The cumulative effect of a variety of similar errors, superficially innocuous as they may be, combined with a number of pointed and persistent misrepresentations, has been to obscure Colbert's real role in the preparations for the rebellion, in the battle itself and even in his court martial and execution. The purpose of this book is to bring as much clarity to these issues as the sources will permit, and to present as realistic a portrait as possible of what type of a person Colbert was. Colbert never consciously cultivated a reputation for himself. Others decided to do that after his execution. To encounter a historical figure is all too often to encounter fiction. The first duty of any biographer should be to afford a subject, and an audience, the appropriate complexity – in this case, to separate the man and the myth. Only then is an honest assessment of a life possible. And it should be for his life as much as for his death that Colbert is commemorated.

The Rising was a spectacular display of resistance to the British empire near the height of its power and on an active war footing. The rebel leaders anticipated that they were striking a decisive blow in a struggle for national liberation. The Proclamation of the Republic invoked a tradition of militant resistance, envisioned an independent Ireland, and proposed a pluralist society resting on an anti-imperial foundation. But this was not a simple story. The political and cultural history of Ireland in the years before 1916, and the history of the Rising itself, remains enigmatic and it would be insensitive and irresponsible to draw simplistic conclusions, whether celebratory or condemnatory, on intricate matters.

While overt republicanism and separatism were fringe phenomena during the first decade and a half of the twentieth century, subsequent events would demonstrate that there was an extensive slumbering sympathy for radicalism that was roused by the Rising. Opposition to continuation of the Union of Great Britain and Ireland with direct government from London was the norm, yet the primary proposal of the nationalist majority was for no more than Home Rule, a limited measure of control over domestic affairs for a Dublin parliament. As well as constitutionalist principles, there was a strand of imperial sentiment running through sections of the Home Rule movement, but its moderate claim reflected realism regarding the balance of power in Anglo-Irish relations, rather than idealistic aspiration or conviction.

Unionists, predominantly Protestant and with their power base in northeast Ulster, feared Home Rule as a threat to their political, cultural, civic, economic and religious interests. The nationalist strategy assumed that when the government eventually conceded a compromise reform, which could not be denied indefinitely, unionists would consent once convinced that it was a benign measure. This gamble, democratic as it was, failed to understand the depth of feeling inherent in the unionist – British – imperial dynamic, and was lost at huge cost. Unionism had evolved from a more conciliatory phase earlier in the century to the point where it resolutely refused any concession. Unionists now demonstrated a readiness to defy the common will and even parliamentary opinion.

When Home Rule legislation was introduced in 1914, proviso was made for the exclusion of Ulster.[1] So it was not because of the Rising that partition reared its head. The concept had already entered the public debate and the precedent had been set: Home Rule, if and when it was enacted, would not apply to the whole country. The onset of world war left an uncertain and uneasy situation hanging in suspended animation.

The relevance of 1916 to all of the island's understanding of its past is acute. Turning the Rising into a historical cult prevents real debate and only baits shallow sensibilities. Defending its ideals does not have to supercede reasonable concerns about its democratic credentials and the appropriateness of the use of physical force. On the other hand, the false reduction of the rebels to nothing more than vacuous fanatics, and the mocking of its commemoration, is a pernicious form of historical politicking and part of a lamentable reaction to latter-day imperatives. The Troubles meant that from the late 1960s, the historicisation of the claim to national self-determination and the nature of Irish state formation became more than purely academic affairs. Historians of the Rising found themselves arbitrating on issues critical to the contemporary conflict, particularly on competing legitimations of government authority, the use of violence to overthrow such authority, and the question of a mandate for such action. The task that some historians set themselves was to reconcile opposition to militant republicanism with the revolutionary origins of the Free State.[2] An essential point, however, is that the 'intimidatory gunman lurking in the shadows' of the Union was British.[3] Britain had never succeeded in fully integrating Ireland into the Empire, and a critical factor in the structure of the Union was the overwhelming superiority of British firepower. Ireland was part of a democracy in 1916, albeit an already flawed one that was further grievously undermined by the extra-parliamentary tactics of Ulster unionism between 1911 and 1914. The rebels did not introduce the gun to Irish politics. It was already present.

Since their executions, the lives and deaths of the sixteen men who form the subjects of this series of biographies have been the playthings of politicians, revolutionaries, journalists and polemicists, as well as historians. Their memories have been hijacked and their legacies appropriated, to be shaped by those with an agenda other than historical objectivity. Approaches have veered wildly between secular sanctification and demonisation. Some commentators have adopted a deliberately derogatory and anachronistic style, in order to challenge those who would justify the persistence of physical-force tradition by reference to the ideology of the Rising and its effect on public opinion. Admirers are charged with knowingly providing succour to undemocratic insurrectionists.

The actions of a small number of individuals, representative perhaps of only a minority, clearly had a profound impact, but the influence of the Rising on subsequent political events and the responsibility or otherwise of its abettors for later violence is not the issue here. The aim is to present a fair and balanced biography of Con Colbert, who was in many ways an ordinary man, but one who did some extraordinary things in extraordinary circumstances. To what degree he played a role in fomenting those circumstances is arguable.

The very fact of his execution has ensured Colbert's continuing historical resonance and relevance. Imagine for a moment that he had not been executed – would he still warrant a biography? Was what he did unique, or were there many who made similar or more important contributions to Irish politics and society in the same period? If he had not been executed, would it have been a glaring omission? How important was the element of chance? The rationale for his execution, and the capricious process behind it, must be examined closely.

Of the sixteen men executed, Colbert is among the lesser known. In the public mind, as in major studies of the Rising, he tends to occupy a peripheral role. Because of his lower profile, he has also not been a target of character assassination. If anything, the opposite has been the case. When he has received sustained or detailed attention, it has been uncritical and unquestioning. He was not one of the seven signatories of the Proclamation. He was not a battalion commandant, but held relatively junior rank. He was not a renowned orator, ideologue or statesman. But his commitment inspired his colleagues. His loyalty and competence won their admiration and gained him the trust of the Military Council of the Irish Republican Brotherhood (IRB), which planned the Rising. There is no shortage of testimony from Colbert's contemporaries as to his disposition and ability, and how these qualities inspired respect, but there are relatively few of his own words by which to judge him along with his actions. He did not leave a diary, and there is no indication that he ever kept one. His poetry was not designed for public consumption. It was somewhat formulaic, and repetitive of standard nationalist imagery. His thematic range was limited. His compositions fit snugly in the genre of romantic nationalism. A representative selection of titles is 'The call of Éireann', 'How to be a patriot', 'To be free' and 'We must be free'.[4] Ireland as mother was a habitual motif. Colbert died at the age of twenty-seven. Of the executed men, only Ned Daly and Seán Heuston were younger. Tom Clarke was three decades older.

Colbert wrote no fewer than eleven letters to family and friends on the night before his execution. There are several accounts of his attitude and conduct at this point, but one should be cautious in drawing wide-ranging conclusions from such an exceptional situation. One record of his trial suggests that he was submissive, and this could be interpreted as Colbert wishing his ordeal of failure to end; a conflicting version suggests that he attempted to assert himself in the face of falsehoods. Three letters to a brother in America, most likely written between 1909 and 1911, do unveil something of the man's character and his thinking on the issues of the day. Unfortunately, letters from his brother to Con do not seem to be extant. However, there is enough evidence in the few letters which survive, as well as in his behaviour, to suggest that the traditional conception and portrayal of Colbert needs to be modified.

Unlikely ever to have considered the possibility that historians would study these documents a century after his death, Colbert displayed more awareness of his own normality and insight into his own flaws than is evident in most fawning secondary accounts. He may not have had many, or perhaps even any, vices, but he did have the usual human concerns about things like money, fleetingly at least. Second-hand testimony suggests that he seems to have agonised over his romantic relationships with women. It might be unfair to say that he had a curious attitude to romance, but he certainly prioritised his public life over his private life. His choices in this regard were, on the surface at least, unusually selfless, and lack of evidence means there is no way to delve deeper. The insights into his character provided by his letters make it much easier to empathise with Colbert the man, as opposed to Colbert the symbol of the Rising.

In a letter dated 6 February, in what the content indicates was probably 1909, Colbert wrote to 'A Seaghan dílis' (Dear John), as he always addressed his brother in California:

I am sorry that you should turn to flattery as a means of complimenting me. I am not eloquent, nor is my patriotism above that of the ordinary man. I try to have a real unselfish love for Ireland but human nature often asserts itself and makes me serve Ireland – sometimes that I might gain fame, at others that it might be a means to the end of serving myself; however I overcome these feelings to as great a degree as I can do; and try to make every action of mine acceptable to the good of my country.[5]

These frank admissions provide a revealing glimpse into the mind of a twenty-year-old who seems somewhat unsure of himself. He is striving to carve out a role. His uncertainty is just as striking as his ambition. His hope is for promotion within the movement, rather than simply self-promotion, and he is struggling to enhance his reputation rather than gain notoriety. This was a balancing act at which he became more adept over the following years.

Michael Madden, who in 1983 produced *Captain Conn Colbert. Defender Watkins' Brewery Marrow Bone Lane Area, Easter Rebellion 1916*, described his work not as a biography but as a 'pen picture'. Characterised by an explicit religious tone, it exemplified the hagiographic approach to the rebels which came into vogue soon after the Rising and held sway in some quarters for several decades. Madden depicted Colbert in messianic terms, and as a martyr:

The man of deep religious faith in daily communication with his God; a man who hated injustice and loved his country and his people; a man who fitted himself mentally and physically for the task of leading his people from Egypt to the Promised Land. A soldier eager not for the glorification of war but for the God-given right to free his country from foreign domination. A captive in the hands of the enemies of his country in bleak and cold Kilmainham Gaol awaiting a martyr's death with belief in the justice of his cause and in God's mercy … I can see God's Son who came on earth to liberate enslaved mankind and who was also immolated unjustly at Eastertide on a gibbet, waiting on that 8th of May morning in 1916 to welcome Con Colbert home at the end of the wearying day.

This account is typical of representations of the executed rebels as 'a band of pure-souled patriots'. Joseph Lawless, a veteran of the Rising, subscribed to this notion:

All, without exception, were governed by a simple honest adherence to the pure ideal of National Freedom. In not one of them was there a hint of mean thought or ulterior motive; but on the contrary, it was abundantly evident that the normal self-interest or concern in personal affairs was placed in a subordinate position in relation to the pursuit of the ideal. … the rank-and-file who strove to emulate the shining example and follow the precept of those whose

direction of the national Cause had to them the appearance
of Divine inspiration.[6]

This passage comes from Lawless' Witness Statement,
submitted to the Bureau of Military History in 1954. The
Bureau's Witness Statements, Volunteers' accounts of their
political and military activities between 1913 and 1921, give
voice to many otherwise silent participants, revealing their
motivations and aspirations. They were recorded in the late
1940s and 1950s and can be problematic in terms of bias,
memory, conjecture, inaccuracy and retrospective justifica-
tion. Furthermore, the process surrounding the creation and
collection of statements was on occasion subject to interfer-
ence from vested interests. Some testimonials were bluntly
prejudiced by personal relations and factional loyalties, but
many are remarkably candid and convey something of the
atmosphere, feelings and emotions of the experience of
being a Volunteer. Comments relating to the leaders of the
Rising were generally gushing in their praise, designed to
lionise the dead men, but the Statements contain valuable
evidence.

Stripping away the effusive accolades, however, it is also
plain that many of Colbert's circle harboured a deep affection for him. Gary Holohan's tribute was all the more sincere
for its simplicity: 'one of my dearest and best friends. Poor
old Con Colbert. Of all the men who fought in the Rising
there was no truer or stouter heart'.[7]

Even before his death, Colbert had been placed on a pedestal as a role model. When Patrick Pearse wished to appoint a bilingual physical education and drill teacher in his school, Scoil Éanna, Colbert was ideally suited on both counts. He held the position from late 1910 to 1916.[8] He declined the offer of a salary, unwilling to accept remuneration for what he considered to be work in the national cause. Colbert apparently reacted with such indignation that Pearse had to apologise and drop the idea of paying him.[9] In *An Macaomh* in May 1913, referring to his regular school staff, Pearse hailed 'gallant Captain Colbert for drill and physical culture'.[10] One of the schoolboys quickly latched on to the compliment. On 24 May 1913, *An Scoláire*, the Scoil Éanna student periodical, carried an open letter to the 'Gallant Captain Colbert':

Friend, So the Macaomh hailed you, proving you a man of worth, as it has paid no compliments to mediocrities. You have done good things in and outside Scoil Éanna. No doubt you will do good things till the day you die. In heaven, I feel sure, you will drill the angels et the saints, not even letting St. Peter off. You understand the grandeur of Ireland. You know the greatness of the task which no one has finished yet. You would ever fight your foes, but never abuse them. The rascals have said before now you are small in size. I pray the Lord to give us more men and women with souls as large as yours.[11]

'Con was on the small side', according to one observer.[12] Colbert's small stature – accounts of his height vary from 5 feet to 5 feet and 4 inches, although his build is almost universally described as 'stocky' – had not gone unnoticed by 'the rascals' in the school, but the author of this piece certainly seemed to have been impressed by the force of his personality.

After the Rising, Colbert was not only a role model, but also a martyr. Political demonstrations were banned, so one manifestation of the growing public sympathy for the Rising and its lost leaders was the phenomenon of memorial masses. As early as 13 June 1916, TP O'Connor recounted to David Lloyd George the quaint tale of one little Dublin girl who successfully called on 'Saint Pearse' to convince her hesitant mother to buy her a new hat. Another apocryphal story O'Connor told Lloyd George was of the priest who, while giving the last rites to Con Colbert and assuring him that he would go to Heaven, begged his intercession to obtain an 'intention', which was 'an unfulfilled though usually secret wish of a religious character'.

> He [the priest] had desired the fulfilment of this 'intention' for many years but [he told Colbert] that if he obtained it within five days after Colbert's execution, he would know that Colbert's intercession had obtained it for him. The 'intention' was realised within three days after Colbert's execution.[13]

The process whereby the spiritual credentials of the rebels and the sacred nature of their cause was emphasised gathered momentum from July 1916, when a popular Dublin magazine, the *Catholic Bulletin*, began a to carry a series of features entitled 'Events of Easter Week', cataloguing, over successive months, the religious qualities of the executed men. The garrisons had frequently recited the rosary and were often visited by priests. Many individuals had prepared for the Rising with devotions over the Easter weekend. Roger Casement converted from Protestantism to Catholicism shortly before his execution, and the other fifteen were all at least nominal Catholics. Some of them had lapsed from practice, including doubting Thomas MacDonagh and sceptical Seán MacDiarmada, but the anti-clerical Fenian Tom Clarke was the only one who did not seek solace in the Church when facing execution.

The piety of the rebels generally was not necessarily exceptional, however, and was probably a fairly representative reflection of the level of religious practice in Irish society at large. The cumulative effect of such uncritical celebration was twofold. Firstly, popular perception came to automatically conflate Catholicism and the Rising, overlooking the non-sectarian and pluralist sentiments of the Proclamation. Secondly, it led to the projection of unrealistic saintly images of the fallen. Volunteer Seán Prendergast reflected on the impact of the *Bulletin* pieces on interned rebels:

To say that we were stirred by the splendid portrayal of good and righteous men would be to use quite a mild term. The few copies that were available in the camp were eagerly sought after, read, and even copied. It would be safe to say that we felt highly honoured by these grand and edifying tributes to our dead leaders.'[14]

Colbert was described as maintaining the highest standards of piety even in the face of his impending demise.[15] His favourite phrase, according to his sister Lila, was 'for my God and my country'.[16] He had been devout, but he was now presented as a symbol or icon of impossibly elevated morality, rather than as a complex human being with flaws as well as virtues, to be judged in the context of his times. He became a personification of the 'faith and fatherland' version of Irish history. In the late 1940s, Madge Daly, sister of Ned Daly and sister-in-law of Tom Clarke, labelled Colbert 'a soldier and a saint'. Because he followed his duty to God and country, she claimed, 'regardless of censure, no matter what the source … he lived and died happily'.[17] Such claims are frequent and have to be scrutinised rather than dismissed out of hand, but they are also part of the propaganda campaign to venerate the dead.

What motivated Colbert to commit himself to violent revolution? What was the influence of his family background and education? Was he ideologically sophisticated or rigidly narrow-minded? How did his mentality change over time?

How was he affected by social factors such as peer pressure? Were his God and his country his only concerns? What kind of a republic was he willing to kill and die for? What did he think would be achieved by the Rising, given the disparity in strength of the respective forces? How did he face his death?

Chapter 1

Home Life and Formative Influences

Cornelius Bernard Colbert was born on 19 October 1888 in Moanlena, Castlemahon, Newcastlewest, in west Limerick. He liked his name, according to his sister Lila, and his siblings usually addressed him as Cornelius, but outside of the family he was generally known as Con. His parents were Michael William Colbert, a small farmer originally from nearby Athea, and Honora (Nora) Colbert (née MacDermott), originally from Cooraclare, County Clare.[18] He was probably named after his maternal grandfather, Cornelius 'Conor' McDermott (1827-1894), who was principal of Cooraclare National School.[19]

His paternal grandparents were William Colbert, a land agent originally from Cork, and his wife Mary (née Condon). William Colbert built and lived in New Park, a house just a few hundred yards outside of Athea, on the north side of the main road from Limerick. This is where Michael William grew up. Con was the tenth of Michael William and Nora's thirteen children, the first eleven of whom were born in Moanlena. The thirteen were William, the eldest, born in 1877 and who emigrated to California; Mary, whose family pet name was Ciss; John, who also went to California; Catherine (Katty); Nora; Johane (Nan), the third of the children to go to California; Michael (Mack), who farmed in west Limerick; Margaret (Gretta); Elizabeth (Lila); Con; Jim, who fought in the War of Independence and later became a Teachta Dála; Dan; and Bridget.[20]

When Con was three years old, Michael William moved the Colberts back to his native place of Athea and built Gale View, a house on the opposite side of the road to New Park, and closer to the village. The second eldest son of William Colbert, he farmed on old family land at Templeathea. William Colbert had left New Park to his eldest son, William Jr., who was a Justice of the Peace and a landlord, as well as a farmer. The 1901 census indicates that five of the neighbouring families in the townland of Templeathea West were tenants of William Jr. He was also the owner of another dwelling, which was unoccupied. According to local and family lore, William Jr. was a 'vain, bossy, autocratic man' and the brothers 'rarely spoke': 'William did not think much of his brother Michael's farming skills nor of his wife Nora's housekeeping skills'.

Con's mother Nora died from 'post-partum haemorrhage' on 17 September 1892, the day of Bridget's birth, but the large family did not separate immediately in response. Con spent some time with relatives in the area, and attended Kilcolman national school while living with his aunt Lizzie at Balliston, near Ballysteen.

Along with three of his brothers and two of his sisters, however, Con was in Gale View at the time of the 1901 census, conducted on 31 March of that year. Despite turning twelve the previous October, Con was recorded as an eleven-year-old scholar. Like everyone else in the house, he could read and write. His father entered his own age as fifty. John, aged eighteen, had finished in school and was working on the family farm. Johane, aged sixteen, had also seemingly finished in school. James, ten, Dan, nine, and Bridget, eight, were all in school.

The walls of Gale View were constructed with stone, brick or concrete, while the roof was thatch, wood or other perishable material. There were five windows in the front of the house and six rooms inside, along with four outbuildings. It qualified as a second-class house. Along the road at New Park, William Colbert Jr.'s house qualified as first-class. It had six front windows and its walls were stone, brick or concrete, while its roof was slate, iron or tile. William Jr., aged forty-five, was married to Norah, aged twenty-nine. They had four sons, aged from one to four. They had six female domestic servants (one of whom was a domestic nurse), and three male farm labourers. There were fourteen rooms occupied in the house. There were twenty outbuildings.

Con's father Michael William died on 12 July 1907, from a form of kidney ailment known as 'Bright's Disease'. William Jr.'s children had a governess until he died from 'cancer of the lower jaw' in 1909. William Jr. was 'pro-British', and Con and he were not on good terms. Reporting on events in Athea to his brother John in San Francisco in early 1909, Colbert revealed the depth of the enmity he felt towards William: 'My uncle is not dead yet – the devil would not kill a bad thing.'[21]

Like the rest of his brothers and sisters, Con received most of his primary education at Athea national school. Maurice Woulfe taught the Colbert children. He was the father of Dick Woulfe, a chemist in neighbouring Abbeyfeale, who was closely associated with the local Volunteers during the War of Independence.[22] Katty Colbert married Dick Woulfe, and their business premises and home in Abbeyfeale was a regular meeting place for republicans. Michael Madden related an anecdote told by Dan Colbert about an achievement of Con's in school: 'Con was in school one day when the Inspector came in … he gave the boys an essay. Con wrote an essay on the River Feale and won First Prize that day'.

In what was almost certainly 1903, Con moved to Dublin

to live with his sister Katty at 7 Clifton Terrace, Ranelagh Road. His first job in Dublin was as an apprentice barman, but this did not last long. He returned to study under the Christian Brothers in 1903, completing the Primary Grade examination at St Mary's Place in 1904, and doing about eighteen months of secondary education at the O'Connell schools, North Richmond Street. Sitting his Junior Grade in 1905, Colbert was awarded honours in English and passed arithmetic, algebra, geometry, physics, French, book-keeping and shorthand. He took night courses at Skerries College for a brief spell, and was apparently called to a post in the Customs and Excise sector of the civil service, but turned down the offer since it would have meant taking an oath of allegiance to the British Crown. Thereafter he commenced to earn his living, obtaining a junior clerkship in Peter Kennedy's bakery in Britain Street (now Parnell Street) in 1905. He studied accountancy for five years through the International Correspondence Schools.[23] He worked for Kennedy's until his death.

He also kept his lodgings at 7 Clifton Terrace until his death. At the time of the 1911 census, on Sunday 2 April, three of the Colbert sisters also lived there. Catherine, a thirty-year-old dressmaker, was head of the household. Lila, aged twenty-three, was a typist in Lafayette's, the photographers. Thirty-one-year-old midwife Ciss had been married for ten years, but was by now widowed. Of three children born alive to her, only one was still living. This was her son James O'Brien, referred to by Con as Bun or Bunnie. It is not clear if James lived with his mother at this point, but he was not at Clifton Terrace on the day of the census. Con was listed as the only one who could speak Irish as well as English. Also present at 7 Clifton Terrace on census day were two boarders. Alfred Dann, a member of the Church of Ireland, was a twenty-one-year-old bank clerk from Tipperary. Ernest Rutter, a thirty-three-year-old Roman Catholic from London, worked as a stationery manager. Emna Dann, Alfred's sister, also boarded at Clifton terrace but was not present on the day.

When Katty moved back to west Limerick in 1913 to marry Dick Woulfe, 7 Clifton Terrace 'was taken over by a friend of ours', according to Lila. This was Maggie Clarke, accompanied by her Volunteer brother Joseph.[24] While Con kept his lodgings at Clifton Terrace until the Rising, Lila moved to new digs at 95 Haddington Road. Nancy and May McDonnell, two sisters who shared with Lila at Haddington Road, later married two of the Colbert brothers. May worked with Lila at Lafayette's. Nancy and Con always conversed in Irish, while Lila and May listened 'without understanding a word'.[25]

Back in Gale View, Con's sister Nora, aged twenty-four, was head of the household and listed her occupation as 'farmer'. Gretta, Michael and Jim lived with her, and they employed an agricultural labourer named Thomas O'Connor. Con, who was twenty-two since the previous October, was listed as twenty-one years old. It seems that there was a general consensus among the Colberts, probably including Con himself, that he was a year younger than was actually the case. Lila, for instance, knew that he was the fourth-youngest child, but did not know exactly what age he was at the time of his execution.[26] Not only his family laboured under a mis-apprehension as to his age, however. One close republican confederate, referring to 1916, estimated that 'Colbert was then about 23 years of age'.[27] Madge Daly suggested that, like Ned Daly and Seán Heuston, the only executed men younger than him, Colbert 'was little more than a boy when he faced the British firing squad'.[28] His boyish looks did nothing to contradict this.

Madge Daly wrote of Colbert as 'hero and martyr':

> … inspired by a patriotic fervour richly inherited from both sides of his parentage. An uncle was out with the Fenians, and his mother was one of the McDermott's of Cooraclare, who were in the vanguard of the national effort since 1882.
> … My uncle had known Con's Fenian uncle, about whom Con was ever anxious to hear.[29]

Michael Madden referred to Colbert's 'Fenian background' and the influence of his uncle Dr John Colbert, 'who held strong Fenian sympathies'.[30] The fact that there was a magistrate and a medical doctor in the extended family, as well as the fact that they were landowners, suggests that the Colberts would have been regarded as 'respectable', which could lead one to deduce that they were relatively well off. This might not have been the case, however, especially with so many children to feed. Writing to his brother John in San Francisco in 1909, Con reminisced about their youth in Athea:

> Well every scene and memory comes back to me now – all about Gael View: 'tho poverty reigned often there, still who were happier than the Colberts? Noble and proud, tho' poor and ragged aye and often hungary. Well God rest those that are gone, they did more than ordinary beings for us under the circumstances.[31]

These circumstances also help to explain the absence of photographs of Colbert as a boy.

With regard to his politicisation, there can be little doubt about which uncle's example Con followed more closely. Many rebels considered themselves as having been born into the Fenian tradition, and felt duty-bound to contribute to the continuation of the physical-force struggle. While many revolutionaries were born into revolutionary families, it might be something of an exaggeration to define the Colberts as such. A second recollection of Dan Colbert's about his brother, however, was that 'Con would often be "missing" at home. Like most lads, he would be found in his favourite hide-out – the turf shed. He would usually be found there reading Irish history.'

His home environment, then, was a force in forging Colbert's national identity, but it did not function in isolation. While nationalists considered the neglect of Irish culture, language and history to be the most serious defect in the education curriculum, it did not stop the cultivation of a distinctly nationalist ethos in many national schools. Like many others involved in the Rising, Colbert's separatist tendencies may well have been confirmed, if not originally inculcated, by his educational experiences, including attendance at Christian Brothers' schools.

Most rebels were instructed in the Fenian tradition, and the teaching of history may have been a factor in transforming a separatist conviction into a commitment to fight. In this context, it is pertinent to reflect on David Fitzpatrick's suggestion that

> Whenever the gospel of nationalism is preached some grow excited, some yawn or look at their watches, some remain preoccupied with farm or family, some snigger or scoff, some hurry to the police barracks. Of those whom the gospel excites, some will remain nationalists for a lifetime, some for a week, and some for the duration of a meeting.[32]

The claim of a link between political violence and interpretations of the past has some validity. Barry Coldrey provided evidence that more past pupils of the Christian Brothers were involved in the revolutionary activity of 1916-21 than could reasonably be expected by chance.[33] Of course, this does not prove that it was the socialisation they underwent at school that turned their minds to militant nationalism, as there is also evidence that parents with strong nationalist convictions tended to send their boys to be educated by the Christian Brothers.

However, it is reasonable to ask to what extent their school experience contributed to their politicisation. Peter Hart also singled out the Christian Brothers as a key formative influence on the development of revolutionary nationalists. The Brothers were associated with the education of the children of lower-middle-class Catholics and skilled tradesmen in urban areas. Coldrey attributed to the Brothers the creation of 'the ideal revolutionary group', namely 'a pool of well-educated lower-middle-class young men' dedicated to nationalist principles. This revolutionary cohort closely correlated to the social profile of the 1916-23 republican Volunteer delineated by Peter Hart: 'In teaching patriotism, the brothers created gunmen.'[34]

Outside of the home and school, political organisations, cultural movements and ideology can all be important radicalising factors and, as Fearghal McGarry put it, 'for the minority that embraced separatism before 1916, a stance that required intellectual independence and moral courage, their very marginalisation reinforced their commitment'. There is a general consensus among historians that the radicalisation of Irish nationalists was significantly influenced by social, economic and communal pressures, but few rebels expressed their commitment in these terms. They concentrated on the outwardly uncomplicated cause of Irish freedom. Their motivation, as they perceived it, was purely patriotism. The centrality of childhood influences seems apparent, but is impossible to quantify. The role of overlapping cultural and separatist networks, particularly in Dublin, is striking.[35]

Like many separatists, socially conservative Catholic Colbert displayed no interest in the potentially divisive dynamics of class struggle. Nowhere did he identify the source of his ideology or communicate it in complex terms, other than to broadly condemn British rule in Ireland as unjust and unnatural. But he did not have to do more than this.

For many people like Colbert, politicisation amounted to resentment of common grievances blamed on London, hostility to everyday manifestations of British power, devotion to Irish culture, and an abstract idealisation of Irish freedom. This was a given for separatists, who identified the union with Britain as an imperialist imposition, the primary source of Ireland's economic, social, cultural and political woes. They assumed its sundering would solve Ireland's problems, and regarded rebellion as a proper assertion of national sovereignty. The 1916 rebels fought the Crown under the banner of the republic. Republicanism, for Colbert at least, was about liberation from occupation and colonisation rather than any specific political programme. The idea of the ethereal republic was a symbol of a free Ireland.

The forceful message conveyed by the mainstream nationalist narrative of the Irish past in the nineteenth century was not of provincial autonomy within the United Kingdom. Rather, it was of a nation with a glorious but as yet unfulfilled destiny of independence. The development of nationalist historical consciousness and identity was shaped by the dissemination of this narrative through popular books, ballads, commemoration ceremonies, iconography, imagery, monuments, newspapers, periodicals and poems. The song most closely associated with the Home Rule movement was 'God Save Ireland', a tribute to Fenian separatists hanged by the Crown.

In the latter decades of the nineteenth century, there was a substantial de facto historical education industry in place outside of the schools. Con Colbert was at least partly a product of this industry. He was probably also at least partly a product of the Catholic devotional revolution of the third quarter of the nineteenth century. Devotional exercises were designed to encourage more frequent participation in the sacraments and to instil piety. The symbolism of populist Catholic religious fervour and nationalism blended seamlessly. Irish republicanism was initially inspired by the Enlightenment Protestant radicalism of Theobald Wolfe Tone and the United Irishmen, but by the early twentieth century, it did not feature to any great extent the anti-Catholicism and anti-clericalism that characterised its continental counterparts.

Nationalism is, of course, a trait of individuals rather than of nations. Not everyone in Ireland was a nationalist, let alone a separatist. Nevertheless, as Joost Augusteijn recognised, by the end of the nineteenth century, a majority of Irish Catholics shared the belief that Ireland was a separate nation held by England against its will. A sense of nationalism and opposition to British rule was commonplace, and while separatist nationalist thinking was continualy being refined, feelings do not have to be supported by a sophisticated ideology. Many wanted an independent Ireland, but not everyone agreed on what form it should take or the means by which it should be achieved, and fewer again were prepared to fight for it. What differentiated Con Colbert from the majority of his peers was his decision to fight. The question is not why he was a nationalist, but why he chose to fight.[36]

Parnell's Irish Parliamentary Party dominated Irish electoral politics before the Rising. The cause with which it was most closely identified, but which it pursued without ultimate success, was that of Home Rule. The Parliamentary Party was perhaps the most representative voice of Irish nationalism and, at least by the measure of voting patterns, its position seemed to be unassailable. There is reason to suspect, however, that this may be a somewhat superficial standard. The grassroots network of the Home Rule movement became gradually less active and increasingly nominal, and there is evidence that local branches were sometimes purely electoral in purpose, existing only on paper and being irrelevant outside of campaign time. This suggests that the position of the Parliamentary Party was much more precarious than has been traditionally portrayed by historians. Its impressive statistics proved to be little more than paper tigers after 1916.[37] While the aging and old-fashioned Parliamentary Party stagnated, a new generation of nationalists was drawn to Irish-Ireland bodies, which were primarily concerned with intellectual and cultural expressions of identity. The Gaelic League and the Gaelic Athletic Association (GAA) highlighted what they considered to be the destructive features of Anglicisation and provided self-confident and popular arguments for the recognition of Ireland as a distinct nation. But while the majority of cultural revivalists did not equate Home Rule with the attainment of real independence and an Irish-Ireland, they continued to vote for the Parliamentary Party until after the Rising. There were hundreds of thousands of members of the Gaelic League and GAA before 1916, but only the most zealous became engaged in separatist violence. The process of radicalisation is quite clear in Colbert's case.

Chapter 2

• • • • •

Cultural Nationalist

Con Colbert was a dedicated Gael and 'for the most committed Gaels', according to Fearghal McGarry, 'cultural nationalism became more a way of life than a pastime, encompassing a moral as well as cultural dimension'.[38] It is difficult to pinpoint exactly when Colbert joined the Gaelic League, which sought to revive Irish as the vernacular of the country. By his sister Lila's reckoning, it would have been in 1905, between when he finished school at North Richmond Street and when he took up his position at Kennedy's bakery:

> He was enthusiastic about everything Irish and had now begun to study Irish. He acquired great proficiency in the language and spoke it fluently. He always bought clothes of Irish manufacture. ... After his execution a cap of his marked – Irish manufactured, Gleeson's a firm in O'Connell St., was found in his locker at Kennedy's.[39]

He was a diligent attender at classes and lectures, and an enthusiastic participant in the League's social as well as cultural and educational activities. Those who came under Colbert's tutelage in Na Fianna Éireann, or were fellow members of the Gaelic League, IRB or Irish Volunteers, were struck by his evident love for the Irish language and associated traditions. Gaels rejected foreign influences in as many facets of their lives as achievable. Colbert's 'soul burned for everything Gaelic and Irish. It would do you good to see him at a ceilidhe', stated Gary Holohan.[40]

Seán Prendergast admired him as 'the very personification of the Gael; [he] spoke the language of the Gael with notable frequency; everything about him was Irish. He always dressed in kilts on parade or assemblies. ... So sincere was he on the question of the native language that he used issue commands in Irish'.[41] Seán Kennedy distinctly remembered him dressing in 'a green jersey with a high collar, kilts, long stockings'.[42] The wearing of kilts by Irish-Irelanders was not uncommon, and could serve a dual purpose, functioning as an authentic Irish 'costume' or a quasi-military uniform as the occasion demanded.[43] Ellen Sarah Bushell, a silk weaver, made kilts for Colbert and Na Fianna from 1910.[44]

Colbert insisted that duty to country involved 'preparing Ireland for England's day of difficulty':

... this preparation consists in making Ireland strong intellectually, physically and industrially. Intellectually by the study of Irish language and literature thus helping to replace the Irish tongue its proper place – as the spoken language of the Irish people. Physically: by playing the games destined to be played by the gael for the development of muscle and sinews of Ireland. And industrially by completely boycotting English goods and buying Irish manufacture whenever obtainable.

For Colbert, Ireland and Irishness, as he perceived it, always contrasted favourably with alternatives. His personal construal of a long history of subjugation manifested itself in an artificially inflated sense of superiority. 'No dance', for instance, was 'as fair as the jig or a reel, the old Irish dance with the toe and the heel ... no dance with it can compare'. He insisted on Ireland's unique lineage, purity and virtue:

> ... a nation famed for its learning and high civilisation when England was ruled by savages ... the Roman, the Dane and the Saxon conquered Britain while Ireland held her ground and liberty free from thraldom ... Ireland was the only known country which Ceasar did not subdue.

An alliance of Catholic and Protestant would see Ireland 'restored to her ancient glory as a great nation – foremost in Science, Art, Learning and Power'. Colbert's poetic fashioning of the ultimate Irishman, 'Conchobar Dubh', was heavily autobiographical. 'Conchobar Dubh' was a fine physical specimen, a champion hurler, a scholar of Irish history, an idealist who worked for freedom with the gospel as his sword.[45]

Christy Byrne and Bob Holland described Colbert as a 'fluent' Irish speaker.[46] Gary Holohan recalled that it was

> ... usual for the Fianna to salute each other in Irish from the first. Con Colbert was a great enthusiast and used the little he had on every occasion. I did learn a word here and there, but the first time I heard Irish spoken properly was when Con Colbert brought me to a Modern College of Irish on a Saturday afternoon about 1915.[47]

It is not clear that Colbert ever achieved mastery of the spoken language. He was inconsistent in the spelling of the routine Irish phrases he used as greetings and farewells in letters to his brother John in San Francisco. A recurring theme in these letters, however, was his concern for the status of the language:

> As regards the Irish language I think that everyone should make an effort to learn all they can of it; of course I know there are some who have little time to devote to the development of their minds but my experience of people in regard to the study of Irish is: that those who have the least time to spare make the greatest effort to learn their mother tongue.

'Try and address your letters in Irish', he urged John in a letter of 9 February 1909. Fresh from his Gaelic League classes, Colbert's enthusiasm for an Irish-Ireland is almost palpable. His political opinions, naturally enough, were heavily coloured by his cultural concerns. He kept a close watching brief on related current affairs, particularly on the campaign to make Irish compulsory for National University of Ireland matriculation, a campaign which started with the foundation of that institution in 1908 and culminated in success in 1911. He outlined his thinking to his brother:

> Sinn Féin is indeed a fine expression, of course you know it means 'ourselves', and as such is the … only truly Irish policy. The Parliamentary Party are doomed: but so foolish are the Irish people, that [it] is possible to kick them today, and make them believe you were their friend tomorrow. At present the country is warming on the University question – a question of whether there shall be as prominent a place for the Irish language as their is for English, Latin & Greek. If you please, the Irish bishops have decided against making it an essential subject, just as Bishops decided in favour of the Union in 1800. Nevertheless I expect the people of Ireland to assert their patriotism to nationality and make the Irish language an essential subject for the University. God Grant it.

Writing of shared acquaintances, it is clear that he was still at this point able to separate his private and political positions:

> The O'Cs are fine & give us a call now and then. Michael, John and Pat are in the D.M.P. [Dublin Metropolitan

Police]. Of course I hate them for their uniform though I like them as friends.

It is not clear how much recent contact there had been between Con and John, or what form it took, because Con was forced to ask, 'What are you doing yourself? – you never told me'. As ever with such letters to emigrants, Colbert wanted to update the exile on mundane daily events at home:

> Athea is getting gay and all are well there. I saw Mrs Dalton and Patsy with their 3 bonny children. She's as gay as ever and will never forget Jack Colbert [this probably refers to John himself]. Jim Hayes made three marches and broke then. He is making a fourth and I think he'll be buckled this time. Bridge is the same Bridge. … I also was to see Margaret Mary she is strong and has a very nice husband and place. She was … there in San Francisco. S O'Donnell was in Athea with me. He is as quick as ever and a great patriot and greater Sinn Féiner.

Con was also clearly concerned with the well-being of the family, and sought his older brother's advice:

> Mack is well. So also are Nora, Gretta & Jim. What will Jim become? It struck me the best thing to do was to put him at some profession or other. I think if he was put at engineering – (mechanical or electrical) that he would be successful. Write and let me know your views regarding him. Katty &

Lila are well. Phil and May often come to see us. They are very happy. Ciss is going for the nursery and Bunnie is with us – as hardy as a rock. Dannie never writes to me but often to home. He is quite well and will be a good man yet … Katty never writes to anybody she has not time – indeed there are little prospects of her getting married as far as I can see [he was to be proved wrong on this]. I will tell her to write to you. Aunt Lizzie, Bridget and Con are very well – Con never takes <u>anything</u> now, thank God. Glad to hear of Nan's success she should be lucky.

Colbert concluded this first letter with a review of his own circumstances in Dublin:

As regards athletics, except a little bit of hurling I never do anything [but he was at a peak of physical fitness when taking the Fianna and Volunteers on 'forced marches' a few years later]. No great chance to develop athletics in Dublin while one is trying to make a living and study. Time will bring us the value of our work. 15/-" a week at 10 hours a day for 6 days of the week is my present salary and work. God increase it is my prayer.

The 'study' that he refers to was probably related to his Gaelic League membership. His hope for divine financial intervention is one that would have been shared by many workers. It is an understandable sentiment. Colbert does seem to have devoted most of his disposable income to nationalist activities, however, and his personal and public lives became increasingly intertwined.

The next letter from Con to John was dated 9 December. Con's reference to the daily *Sinn Féin* newspaper, which ran for six months before being abandoned in January 1910, and to the recent establishment of a 'boys National organisation' [Na Fianna was founded in August 1909], indicates that the year was 1909. The slightly awkward opening section indicates that there has not been regular contact between the two. The tone becomes more relaxed, however, as Con inquires about both siblings and family friends who have also left Athea for the same area of California as John:

> It is well nigh time that I had heard from you, or you from me. In truth I don't know which of us it was wrote last, however it doesn't matter much. If it be I, well all I can say is 'I'm sorry' and all I can do is to try and make up for it in this letter which I shall try to make interesting. Where will I begin? What shall I say? Well. I hope this letter finds you in the best of health and highest prospects of prosperity. How is Nan, and Willie and family. Fine of course. Willie did not answer my last letter. Too busy I suppose. Nan is a lucky girl. I hope she shall do well. What about Tommie Danaher and Bride. How are they battleing with their new state in a new country? And Mike Hayes is he well? I don't know of any others, if there be, well I hope they are in their best.

Moving the focus to family members in Dublin and in Limerick, Con is forthright about how they find themselves:

Now Katty and Lila are very well, as is Ciss and Bun. Katty works very hard as usual and Lila is studying and working. Ciss is a trainee midwifery nurse now and is at present down in Carlow on a case. She is likely to do very well. She never touches the uisge beatha [whiskey] now. While she keeps so, there is no fear; and with God's good help she will [Ciss had been widowed and lost two children]. Bun is going to school every day, he would make a bright lad, but he does not study much. Poor chap, he's as wild as the horses that you hunted with 'White Eye'. Do you remember her, and how you couldn't shoot her in the glen. … All in Gael View have surely a good time, tho' colds are rampant there. Mack is at home and training some hurlers. Jim is roaming over the country on horseback while Gretta is getting a pony trained to drive her out. Norah is as usual and Bridgie is going to school every day.

Again, Con blends the personal and the political when he once more seeks John's advice on the education of a sibling, in this case their youngest sister, and draws a link to one of the great public debates of the day:

You should write a letter to Bridgie and ask her mind her books. We would try and give her a good education for she is the only one left. Also ask her mind her Irish – as it is

53

becoming more than a patriotic movement now, and soon there won't be a situation open in Ireland where Irish won't be compulsory. A great fight is at present being raged over the University question. This fight has raged all this year and will never cease till Ireland's language gets its rightful place among the languages of the world in their own University. Everything points to a return to the paths of national spirit now. We have a Sinn Féin daily paper and it is doing wondrous work.

This is Colbert's second reference to Sinn Féin, and while there is no evidence that he was a member of any branch of the party, he was closely following their work. His political commentary has become more radical over the course of 1909. In this letter of 9 December, excited by the formation of Na Fianna, he makes his first allusion to militant resistance to British rule:

Ten years time and Ireland will be ripe for a struggle with the cursed robbers who change this country into a desert from its great fertility. Now I have to tell you that we've started a boys National organisation, where they are taught war tactics, and when the day will come they will be able to show the stuff that's in them. I am studying Irish myself pretty hard.

Idioms such as 'cursed robbers', 'desert', and 'great fertility' suggest that he has absorbed more nationalist dogma from his Gaelic League classes or from the pages of *Sinn Féin*. The League disseminated the belief that the decline of the language was not even partly the result of a natural process of decay, but exclusively because the British had founded the primary schools in 1831 as a calculated and successful attack on Irish.[48]

Con also emphasises to John, 'For Goodness' sake don't give any money to that political reprobate T.P. O'Connor who is only an Irishman in speech and a pro Englisher at heart.' O'Connor left Ireland in 1870 for a career as a London journalist, and was from 1883 the leader of the Irish Parliamentary Party in Great Britain. He sat at Westminster from 1880 until his death in 1929. He was personally close to leading Liberal and Labour figures, and was heavily involved in fundraising in America. O'Connor's world was very much an Anglo-American Anglophone one. It was far removed from the type of idealised Gaelic society which Colbert seemed to picture for an independent Ireland. John Colbert may have mentioned to Con that he was considering supporting O'Connor in one of his campaigns, and Con is clearly warning him off. The pejorative terms he employs to describe O'Connor indicate that Colbert considered him to have been corrupted both politically and in terms of national identity.

Colbert's sense of Irishness was framed by the writings of Gaelic revivalists, including Pearse, who tended to romanticise and even mythologise the rural west of the country. This provided a yardstick against which to measure contemporary Ireland, drowning as they saw it in a rising tide of Anglicisation.[49] That Colbert was concerned about the calamity of the wasting of the west and about the plight of those forced to emigrate in search of employment is clear from his ode to Achill Island:

Shame is on you men of Éireann
Not yet have you heard the wail
Of the starving ones of Achill
The last stronghold of the Gaedheal.
Hear you not the cries of women
Hear you not the helpless call
Of the children who to Scotland
are forced to go at Harvest's call.
Know you not the insult offered
Know you not the treatment there
(to those so) mild and gentle
Who've come from Achill fair.
Know you not the fate before them
Work like slaves and starve as well
Worse than e'en their fearful housing
Is their company from Hell.[50]

Colbert may have selected Achill as the antidote to what he regarded as the 'West British country' of Dublin because he visited the island on a Gaelic League excursion. Or it might simply have been a stock choice for a poet wishing to venerate the people and landscape of a predominantly Irish-speaking area as a cultural and linguistic repository of true Irishness, a bastion against foreign erosion. His observation that the working and living conditions of the islanders who harvested potatoes in Scotland were only further disimproved by 'their company from Hell' speaks to widespread fears about the nefarious influence of proselytism among emigrant Catholic labourers.

Colbert was a resident of Dublin, the 'second city' of the empire, but one with the worst housing conditions of any city in the United Kingdom and a significantly higher death rate than London. There is no indication that he had the same empathy with urban poverty as he did with rural decline. In a lament, 'Away From Home', written during a burst of poetic activity in the spring and summer of 1909, he sighed 'Oh my heart would be light if I could but live in that loveliest of spots – sweet Temple Athea'.[51] In another offering from that period, 'Waiting at Grafton St', Colbert satirises not only the attitude of some of his fellow Irish citizens to the Lord Lieutenant, Lord Aberdeen John Hamilton-Gordon, and his wife Ishbel Maria Marjoribanks, but also her public health campaigning:

> We're waiting here to see
> The Representative of Royalty
> In this West British country
> Waiting, weary waiting to see him pass

For 'tis plain to be seen
We're the grovelling shoneen
Who'd crawl to see Aberdeen …
… Like his lady as you know
Cures consumption so we're waiting to see him pass
One look from Aberdeen
Or his lady's smile serene
Will make consumption clean

Tuberculosis, or consumption as it was known, killed 12,000 people annually in Ireland, many of them in Dublin city where the disease spread rapidly through vast, overcrowded tenement slums.[52] Germ theory was poorly understood, and tuberculosis was popularly thought to be hereditary. Lady Aberdeen fronted education and eradication programmes by the Women's National Health Association and the National Association for the Prevention of Tuberculosis. Her success in contributing to reducing the number of fatalities caused by the illness was not matched by her efforts to negotiate the political schisms in Ireland. *Sinn Féin* accused her of inventing the tuberculosis crisis and some nationalists characterised her initiatives as modern souperism. Detractors like Colbert mocked her as 'Lady Microbe'.[53]

After December 1909, two full years passed before the next letter from Con to John. Con spent these years, 1910 and 1911, immersed not only in the cultural nationalist movement, but also in Na Fianna and the IRB. Apart from a brief introduction and leave-taking, which are themselves a strange blend of the heartfelt and the somewhat cursory, the letters are largely impersonal. There is no news given or requested, and little evident curiosity as to how his brother is faring. The subject is not Athea, family or friends. Instead, the subject is Ireland, and what Con considers as its brave past and glorious future. In 1909 he had written that Ireland would be 'ripe for a struggle' in ten years. In 1911, having overseen much progress in Na Fianna, he optimistically anticipates that military conflict will ensue 'before too many Xmas's pass'.

Clearly present is an Irish nationalist version of the type of jingoism that was rampant around Europe in the years before 1914, and to which Colbert was evidently not immune. The tone is strident, even shrill, and the rhetoric employed might be more usually found in a polemical pamphlet than in a Christmas letter to a brother. It is the type of rhetoric that he has been listening to at secret meetings or delivered from public platforms, that he has been reading in the advanced nationalist press, and that he has been preaching to his Fianna troops:

Just to hear from the land of your fathers would be hard especially around Xmas; when memories of the past must be ever present. I bear you a message of joy, a message of hope for the old dear land. They, who thought that Ireland's spirit was dead, will soon [see] that Ireland can produce armed men. England sowed well and widely the seeds of Brutality lawlessness and Godlessness and the corn is growing and the grain of revenge is deepening. Hope on! You who would doubt of Ireland's future. The Golden West may be a great land, a rich land, a free land, but the land of the Star Spangled Banner has never struggled for centuries for freedom; It has never given the world a record written in blood like ours; and the glow of an Irish nation shall yet light the world; and before that brightness shall dim all the glory of other nations. Hope on! All who have a drop of blood to shed, and prepare you, who are willing to spill it in the struggle for freedom. Are there no rifles in America. Is [there] no such thing as the 69th or Clann na nGaedheal. Hope on! Since the glow of the dawn is warming the veins of Ireland's youth, and the rumble is the tide of the swollen torrent of bloody tyrants being crushed beneath the heels of the victors. Ireland's alive! Ireland's a great land, none other like it. Ireland's making ready again for another fight and let us pray that that the fight will be won. England may beat us but we'll have given the world another example of what's freedom, whats Ireland and who the Irish are. Lift up your heads oh sons of the Gael and prepare you the way for battle. That's my message. Let it be heard in the west wherever Ireland's sons have ears to hear; that's my Xmas greeting. Roe O'Donnell escaped from the clutches of England at Xmas Eve and perhaps Ireland shall wring herself free from the same greedy grasp before too many Xmas's pass. Hope On! is my message. God save and guard you and all the true sons of the Gael is my prayer. All die, men have as good a chance of heaven on the battlefield as on the Gallows and the chance on the Gallows is as great as that on bed. Which place is nobler. Let young Ireland answer and the west will echo. Love, blessings and happiness be yours this Xmas is the fervent wish of your loving Bro.

Reading between the lines, it is possible to detect something akin to an unconscious insinuation, an unwritten censure to John for abandoning Ireland and the cause. This sentiment generally is to the fore in Colbert's poem, 'In Exile':

I have betrayed my trust
For I have fled from my native land
All for the sake of golden dust[54]

Of particular significance are Colbert's comments to John on what he perceived to be the likely nature and outcome of the future fight for freedom. He wishes for victory but realises the possibility, and perhaps even the probability, of defeat. The overriding imperative, however, is the declaration in arms of Ireland's national rights and character; that 'we'll have given the world another example of what's freedom, whats Ireland and who the Irish are'. It is the kind of message, of rebellion constituting a redemptive act in itself, which Pearse did not offer until a few years later. The letter is evocative of the sense of historical responsibility felt by Colbert and his peers to the physical-force tradition, and which would be expressed in the 1916 Proclamation:

> In the name of ... the dead generations from which she receives her old tradition of nationhood, Ireland ... summons her children to her flag and strikes for her freedom. ... In every generation the Irish people have asserted their right to national freedom and sovereignty: six times during the past three hundred years they have asserted it in arms. Standing on that fundamental right and again asserting it in arms in the face of the world, we hereby proclaim the Irish Republic as a Sovereign Independent State, and we pledge our lives and the lives of our comrades-in-arms to the cause of its freedom; of its welfare; and of its exaltation among the nations.

In reflecting on the prospect of demise in battle or execution as a prisoner, Colbert has come to the conclusion that death as a result of action, even if it results in defeat, is more noble than inaction. There is a striking awareness of the power of symbolism. He wrote elsewhere of 'Éire dear':

> My first desire is the joy of dying for thee
> The honour of death with your cause –
> or life with thee free

The overblown emotionality of such declarations should be set against examples of more clinical, detached thinking:

> If we dare to rise as rose before the men of ninety-eight
> Without a plan to act upon, the gallows is our fate

Consideration of these attitudes is crucial to understanding Colbert's frame of mind immediately before and during Easter week 1916, and when trying to interpret his reaction to surrender, trial and imminent execution. The Rising was still several years away, however. The intervening period was not spent solely in military planning, but in broad and unstinting effort on several fronts. 'If your work seems great', he urged his compatriots in 'An Appeal', which remained unpublished, 'do not falter':

> … for what revolution can be wrought without hard work and determined untiring energy in and whole-hearted devotion to the cause. For Ireland's sake begin now and do the little or the much you can do – suffer for her sake – for no nation was ever freed without suffering and persecution and the lives of many of her sons: therefore do not be chary about your comfort or your life in so great a cause as Ireland's. As it is worth struggling for we must not fear anything that comes. God will help us if we help ourselves.

Duty to country and duty to God went hand in hand in Colbert's mind, and could bind all Irish people together against a common foe:

> He who fears to struggle in a rightful cause is a coward; and he [who] will not struggle in such a cause as ours – the obtaining of liberty for Ireland – is a knave or an idler. Our cause is wrapped up in our religion, and our religion is our cause. No matter whether we be catholic or protestant we are undeniably attached to the Irish cause, for Ireland is the most religious country in the world while England is reputed to be the contrary: therefore no man or woman can regard England with reverence and Ireland with contempt without honouring the ungodly and despising God's religious implanted land. Then let no man or woman tell you he or she is a good catholic or a good protestant if he works not for the liberty of Ireland because God implanted patriotism among the virtues of men as well as he gave each man a duty to do: then every one by God's law is bound to do his duty, and what Irishman's duty does not partly consist in serving Ireland. No Irish person who is not true to Ireland, is not true to duty, and he or she [who] is not true to duty is not a child of God for the work laid out by God for him or her to do is left undone and consequently we are not true to God's service, which is His service as a catholic or protestant.

Revolution was neither a secular nor a sectarian enterprise for Colbert. Ireland even held out the hope of redemption or salvation to her guardians:

To serve her holy rights and laws
To give a hand, her to defend
To give your life for life's cause
A day will come – aye not far off
When back to mother earth you'll go
The hand of death shall on you come
And strike – be you high or low
Think well! Think now of all you do
And how you while your life away
For she shall question you
When from this life you've come away
And she shall ask of one and all
'Have you served me to that degree
I gave you talent brains and power
That you might serve me faithfully
Have you spent a useful life
A life entwined with love for me
Duty – have you nobly done
Answer – 'til eternity'
Happy will those be – who answer can
And look their mother in the face
'I've served you well and loved you too
I nobly ran your noble race
I come to claim a place here
Among the gallant martyred throngs

Who strove with main and might for you

To right your foul and cruel wrongs'

But those who answer dare not make

Nor look their mother nobly

But carve and beg as cowards and knaves

And moan excuses loathly

Oh! hard will she look on all of these

That have no duty nobly done

But ran the pace of an alien race

No life's race has proudly won

'I am proud my son of you who fought

And bled and nobly died

To stop the ebbing blood from flowing

And staunched my wounded side

Come to my breast I love you son

As you in life loved me

A place is here prepared for you

This heart of mine is open for thee'

But you who me disgraced and robbed

And scoffed at my fallen state

Who did not give wither hand or heart

You beg and crave – the day is late

Go – from my side – whence you sprang

And find a little earth away

To mix with, for surely you

Are merely but dirt and clay[55]

• • • • •

Chapter 3

Na Fianna Éireann

Bulmer Hobson made a crucial intellectual and organisa-tional contribution to developing a revolutionary net-work in Ireland between the turn of the century and 1916. From a Quaker background, he was interested in the ideals of civic republicanism and promoted the concept of 'moral insurrection', in which passive resistance was complemented by a readiness to implement guerilla warfare but only in the event of either likely success or a government clampdown.[56]

As well as advancing political bodies such as the Dungan-non Clubs, Cumann na nGaedheal and Sinn Féin, he was instrumental in reinvigorating the IRB, with Tom Clarke and Seán MacDiarmada. One of his earliest initiatives had been the foundation of Na Fianna Éireann, in Belfast in 1902. Na Fianna, in Irish mythology, were the followers of the hero Fionn MacCumhaill. Hobson's Belfast model, however, was a hurling club rather than an attempt to recreate Na Fianna of old.

Due to lack of funding and Hobson's other commit-
ments, the club lapsed. He moved to Dublin in 1908 and
the following year, along with fellow Protestant nationalist
Countess Constance Markievicz, inaugurated the version of
the movement in which Con Colbert enrolled. Inspired by
the legendary warrior band of Gaelic Ireland, the purpose of
Na Fianna was 'to re-establish the independence of Ireland'.
It would achieve this by 'the training of the youth of Ireland,
mentally and physically ... by teaching scouting and military
exercises, Irish history, and the Irish language'. Members had
to declare that: 'I promise to work for the Independence of
Ireland, never to join England's armed forces, and to obey
my superior officers.'[57]

Cultural nationalism mixed easily with traditional republican ideology in Na Fianna, and Colbert was an exemplary
officer, a role model for the younger boys. History was taught
to Na Fianna, 'so that the boys may learn what are the rights
of their country and how those rights must be attained'.[58]
Lectures stressed Ireland's glorious past, the daring exploits
of the Fianna, 'the coming of the English and their destruction of our Irish industries, and the methods they had been
using for almost seven hundred and fifty years to destroy
our Irish language and culture';[59] 'Here was instilled into
our useful minds the hatred of the Sassenach ... we longed
for the day when we too might join in the fight against
the common enemy';[60] 'I was taught that Ireland had never

got anything from England and could never expect to get anything except by physical force'.[61] The broader intellectual context of this indoctrination was a project to script a narrative that would inspire confidence in the Irish capacity for self-government, establish Ireland's equal status with other nations, inspire action and legitimate independence.

This Irish-Ireland emphasis became increasingly pronounced and could lapse into open Anglophobia. Directed by Markievicz, the boys 'staged several plays of Irish character, all helping to revive the love of Ireland and the hate of England again in the Irish people and generally rouse the rebel spirit'.[62] Colbert was a member of Na Fianna players. Their first production was 'The Saxon Shilling'.[63] Gary Holohan soon found himself gravitating towards all things Irish-Ireland:

> We were taught to be aggressive to the RIC, and the boys in Camden Street would avail of every opportunity to attack the Protestant Church Boys Brigade, who at that time were strong and would carry the Union Jack.[64]

Despite Holohan's somewhat menacing tone, the Protestant leadership of the mainly Catholic Fianna protected against the scourge of tribalism. The Boy Scouts, established by British army officer Robert Baden-Powell in 1908, were the most prominent Anglicised or imperial parallel to Na Fianna in Ireland, and Na Fianna was, at least in part, a conscious nationalist reaction to their growing popularity.[65] Markievicz, in particular, was anxious that Na Fianna would be a force for Gaelicisation. Hobson increasingly came to see it as a recruiting ground for the IRB, and a counterpoint to the efforts of the Baden-Powells on behalf of the British army.

The fundamental appeal of this style of organisation lay in the uniforms and military training. One boy crossed the lines from the Baden-Powells to Na Fianna for their more attractive regalia and swords.[66] For another youngster, Na Fianna's French bayonets 'enhanced our status and made us feel like the real thing'.[67] The Union Jack, a powerful symbol as demonstrated during monarchical visits in the early 1900s, was a favoured prize of Na Fianna, and forays into rival territory were not uncommon, with Baden Powell scout camps a regular target.

Colbert himself, accompanied by his brother Jim, once entered a Baden-Powell campsite and tore down their flag, apparently proclaiming, 'That's not our flag, it's foreign and should not be flown in this country.' This was despite the fact, according to Lila Colbert, that 'the boy scouts were all much bigger fellas than the Fianna'. Colbert was known to the Baden Powell leaders. They reported the incident to the police, and he eventually received a summons, which he ignored. In his absence, he was bound to the peace for twelve months. Two years later, in 1913, Colbert and Seán Heuston were leading manouevres near Rathfarnham when some boys were arrested. One of their number, Seamus Pounch, admired his companions, 'mere juveniles', who retaliated against the local RIC barracks and smashed windows with stones.[68]

There were clear similarities between the Fianna ethos and the educational approach implemented by Patrick Pearse in Scoil Éanna, which he had opened just a year earlier in 1908. Pearse aimed to instil a love of things Irish in his students, rather than merely tailoring their learning to employment opportunities in the British empire. He wished to foster what he understood to be a heroic spirit. Pearse's patriotic message was intertwined with the legends of boy-heroes, in particular the fabled Cúchulainn, whose image graced the walls of the school.

Pearse fundamentally believed that Ireland needed not only political independence, but also the promotion of knowledge of the national past in the school system, in order to counter the effects of mental and cultural colonisation. He argued that the education system, as a vehicle of cultural imperialism, deliberately neglected indigenous material, and was 'the most grotesque and horrible of the English inventions for the debasement of Ireland'.[69] The result, according to Pearse, was cultural slavery. Liberation lay in the development of a sense of national identity and the reassessment of basic civic principles. When Pearse took up the sword as well as the pen, his ideological stance was designed to justify political struggle. The potency of his message was apparent in 1916, when several students fought alongside Pearse in the Rising. Pearse, along with his brother Willie, Con Colbert, Joseph Plunkett, and Thomas MacDonagh, who had all taught in some capacity at Scoil Éanna, ultimately faced firing squads for their roles in the uprising.

Patrick Pearse has been branded as bloodthirsty, and it is easy to see how some of his more pungent rhetoric could have attracted such a label. But he was a propagandist rather than a military policy-maker. He occasionally reached an unnervingly fevered pitch of detached enthusiasm about bloodshed. In the wake of the killing of unwitting civilians by the British Army during a Volunteer gun-running episode in Dublin in August 1914, he referred in a private letter to the movement and the country being 'rebaptised in blood shed for Ireland'. At Christmas 1915, the slaughter of the war was his focus in a public article:

> It is good for the world that such things should be done. The old heart of the earth needed to be warmed with the red wine of the battlefields. Such august homage was never before offered to God as this, the homage of millions of lives given gladly for love of country.[70]

The above is probably among the most extreme examples of the language he used in attempting to impel action and to establish the right to rebellion. It should not be taken as widely representative – it did not find favour with the anti-war element in republican circles. Similar bombast was common in contemporary Europe. Writing on the mass carnage of the battle of the Somme, only months after the Rising, English war correspondent Philip Gibbs declared that, 'It is a good day for England and France. It is a day of promise in this war, in which the blood of brave men is poured out upon the sodden fields of Europe'.[71]

Scoil Éanna and Na Fianna, while distinctively Irish in their particular motivation and application, were not unique in their concentration on values of social responsibility, self-respect, self-discipline and masculinity. They operated in a Gaelic nationalist rather than imperial context, but they had their roots in contemporary international fears shared among heavily militarised societies about the moral decline and physical readiness of the next generation, so many of whom, volunteers and conscripts alike, were to be sacrificed in the 1914–18 war.

Such anxieties had produced a proliferation of similar militaristic youth factions in Britain and around Europe in the late nineteenth and early twentieth centuries.[72] In England in particular, there had been reservations about the masculinity and virility of the nation's manhood since the end of the Boer War in 1902. Boer victories had prompted concerns about the physical degeneration of the population at large, and medical reports questioned the fitness of a high proportion of men for service in the armed forces. Physical and moral weakness were thought of as symbiotic – where you found one you would automatically find the other. A solution was deemed necessary, not only for military and labour reasons, but for the maintenance of social order also.

As is so often the case, primary responsibility for resolving a perceived societal ill was placed squarely on the education system. Under direction from the Board of Education, acting in tandem with the War Office, schools were increasingly obliged to provide physical exercise for students. The response in Ireland was generally slow, but Scoil Éanna was one of those institutions that bucked the trend. The programme implemented under Colbert's tutelage was known as the Swedish Method. It advocated militaristic drilling, marching and responding to formation commands.[73]

Colbert was already employing similar techniques with Na Fianna Éireann. He attended the inaugural meeting of Na Fianna on 16 August 1909 and, displaying the same industriousness and meticulousness as he did in the Gaelic League, soon accumulated influence. His initial appointment was as captain. He impressed in instructing Fianna classes in drill, small arms, signalling, scouting, map reading and first aid, as well as in leading field manoeuvres. A keen Fianna recruiting agent, much of his summer holidays were spent cycling through the country, especially around Limerick, seeking new supporters.[74]

He was fastidious about his dress and appearance, and tried to instil this trait in Fianna members. Bob Holland recalled how Colbert stressed the importance of personal hygiene: 'He often lectured boys on how they should keep their bodies. He used to tell them that they should wash their feet as often as they washed their face.'[75] Colbert had 'a very dramatic way of speaking'[76]. It seems reasonable to assume that he spoke with a west Limerick accent and, judging by Dubliner Holland's reference to his 'broad brogue', that he never lost it.[77]

Separatist republicanism defined itself in ethical as well as in ideological terms, and Na Fianna emphasised the importance of morality, but, unlike other youth groups of the period, rarely made reference to religion. This was probably because Hobson and Markievicz, as well as recognising how politically divisive religion was in Ireland, did not want Catholic parents to suspect proselytism where none existed.[78] Deeply personally pious, Colbert was a daily communicant and 'a very good-living Catholic' according to Holland.[79] He did not curse.[80] He did not eat meat during Lent.[81] Ardently ascetic, Colbert was a non-smoker and did not drink alcohol, joining the Pioneer Total Abstinence Association in 1906.[82]

While he seems to have been driven by a moral as well as a political imperative, his teetotal lifestyle and his emphasis on personal discipline may have been inspired by his reading and interpretation of Irish revolutionary history. On one occasion, when Major John MacBride lectured to Na Fianna on the military aspects of insurgent movements, Colbert challenged his assertion that drunkenness led to indiscipline and defeat. In Colbert's view, it was a lack of discipline that led to drunkenness rather than the other way around.[83] Holland suggested that his sole ambition was 'to free Ireland', and that this consumed him:

> In fact he never spoke about anything else unless it was connected with Irish History and all his lectures centered around the subject of 'Why we failed'. His answer to this question was always 'Drink and want of discipline and loose talk'.[84]

It is likely that the Fianna maxims of 'purity in our hearts, truth on our lips, strength in our arms' appealed strongly to Colbert.

Seán Prendergast's first impression of Colbert was of a 'bold, serious type':

> In course of time, however, I had reason to form the opinion that notwithstanding a seemingly hard exterior or appearance, he was of a gentle kind and considerate nature. He carried himself with a proud, confident and military bearing, and took his work very seriously. Zealous and enthusiastic in our cause, he expected all similarly engaged to be likewise. He was reputed to be one of our best officers, had great command of himself and was always worthy of being

obeyed. Con was not the type that could be satisfied by doing things by halves or any old way. He sought perfection in every part of his work on behalf of the Fianna.[85]

To become proficient at military drill, for instance, he employed a British army instructor for private lessons on Sunday mornings.[86] Seán O'Neill's single meeting with the 'rather small dark-haired boy, with the eye of a seasoned veteran' was enough to convince him that Colbert was 'a keen, energetic sort of genius who meant business, business without frills, and that alone only for Ireland'.[87]

Lila Colbert's assessment of her brother's attitude echoed that of Holland and Prendergast:

he took his work for the Fianna and the Volunteers very seriously and spent all his spare time at it. He cycled all over Ireland organising companies. I remember he inspected the Company at home in Athea and there is no fear that he showed them any more favour than he did to any of the others. He was very serious where work for Ireland was concerned.

Away from the national movement, he applied himself diligently to his personal development:

When he was at school he felt he had to do his very best at his lessons. And when he worked at Kennedy's he thought he should improve his position in the best way possible, so he devoted himself to the study of accountancy. He did not waste a moment and no matter how late he went to bed, he would make sure to get up in time by tying the alarm clock to the head of his bed. He had to be at work at Kennedy's at 8 o'clock.[88]

The alarm clock certainly seems a more likely explanation for his punctuality than the one Colbert himself apparently gave to Seán Brady:

I asked him how he managed to get up early in the morning when he gave himself so little sleep. 'I'll tell you', he said. 'Before getting into bed, I kneel down and make a bargain with a neglected soul in purgatory. If I awake at the required time, I'll pray fervently for that soul. It never fails, even if I have only a few hours sleep'.[89]

His usual earnestness did not mean that he was a dour character, however: 'he was always full of life and fun. He was constantly making jokes'.[90] Colbert was so happy to see Liam Mellows after his release from a term of imprisonment that 'they spent the night singing rebel songs … they also had pillow fights; nobody got to sleep that night'.[91] Sean Brady acknowledged Colbert's staid side, but also recognised that he was

… active, full of life and fun, and his laughter was delight-
ful. … He visited us quite often, late at night, and usually

in kilts. He was a great favourite with every member of the family, and had everybody laughing with his lighthearted fun and drollery. When he started home, I usually went to see him part of the way home. I enjoyed his company at these times, as his conversation became serious – usually about the hopes and prospects of the future. On the surface it seemed so hopeless … Yet Con knew that, quietly behind the scenes, a determined dedicated few were preparing to challenge that formidable empire.[92]

It was perhaps this sense of assurance, this clarity of purpose, that made Colbert 'a happy energetic man with a great penchant for argument and conversation into the early hours of the morning', as an erstwhile colleague in Kennedy's remembered him.[93] Madge Daly characterised Colbert as 'calm and happy'. She was impressed by his 'kind and unselfish nature. He was ever bright and cheerful and I can never recall seeing him out of humour.'[94]

His trustworthiness and generosity contributed to his popularity, and he was well-respected in Na Fianna and in the Volunteers. 'All his pocket money went for equipment', at a time, according to Holland, when his wages were 27*s*. 6*d*. a week. Colbert's prayer for a raise seems to have been answered, but he still had very little to spare after paying for his digs. 'You could never doubt anything he would tell you and he was never abusive.'[95] His strongest censure was to label one a 'pick axe'.[96] He was reliable and discreet, and 'would not tell his secrets even to his mother'.[97]

Despite his small stature, Colbert seems to have been possessed of an intense physicality. Seán Brady described him as a 'hardy block of a lad, tough as nails … He had a keen, bright eye, and extraordinary energy.'[98] Gary Holohan rated his build as 'powerfully strong', Seán Prendergast as 'muscular'.[99] Lila Colbert admired his 'unbounded energy' and his ruddy good health: 'The only time I remember him being ill was when he had the measles at Clifton Terrace … As he was grown-up he got them rather bad and was very ill.'[100] This was in the last days of 1908 and Colbert spent the New Year period in Athea: 'I was ordered to the country by the doctor who attended me for <u>measles</u> which I got on the 27th of Dec '08', he told his brother John.[101] Seamus Pounch recalled Colbert's 'great strength' and stamina. They clashed in a wrestling bout at one point, and in an impromptu bout of boxing, which was apparently a prominent feature of Fianna training:

> He had no knowledge of the game at all; the round lasted
> five minutes non-stop and at the end I was exhausted. He
> was a little dynamo and attacked with terrific energy from
> start to finish.[102]

William Christian mentioned Colbert being known as 'Cruitur', but did not explain the origins of the nickname.[103] It is not referred to anywhere else, however, and there is no reason to think that it was widely used. Speculating, one could suggest that 'Cruitur' is a version of 'creature', as people who are perceived to be in some way frail are sometimes referred to. In this case, it might have been an ironic allusion to the contrast between Colbert's boyish, innocuous appearance and his physical prowess and military aptitude.

On Saturday, 14 August 1909, both *Sinn Féin* and *An Claidheamh Soluis* carried a recruiting notice for a new 'National Boy's Brigade':

> A meeting will be held on Monday next [16 August] at 34 Lower Camden St. to form a National Boy's Brigade. The Brigade will be managed by the boys themselves on national non-party lines. One of the objects of the new society will be the teaching of the national language and history. Any boy who wishes to work for Ireland is invited to be present at eight o'clock.

Pádraig Ó Riain and Con Colbert were 'the two people who seemed to be most active on that [first] night'.[104] To provide a venue, Markievicz personally rented a hall at 34 Lower Camden St., previously the home of the Irish National Theatre Society (todays's Abbey Theatre). On the night of the first meeting, a boy was posted outside on the street holding a huge green flag with a harp on it to act as a marker or incentive.[105] Pádraig Ó Riain's colleague at *An Claidheamh*

Solais, Seamus MacCaisin, was uneasy in the surroundings: 'there were a number of urchins around … We did not like the look of the place'.[106] Fifteen-year-old Michael Lonergan was one of what he estimated to be fifty or sixty boys, 'mostly adventurers from the Coombe and neighbourhood', who had found their way to the 'dingy hall'. Lonergan found himself 'seated beside a lad whom I judged was not from Dublin at all by reason of his accent, Con Colbert.'[107]

An Céad Sluagh, the first Fianna troop, was formed on the night, with Colbert as its captain and Camden Street as its base. Members adopted a jersey and kilt as their uniform, and the troop had its own pipe band.[108] Other troops wore breeches, and a tunic with brass buttons.[109] An objection was raised at the meeting to women having any part in the organisation. Hobson had to explain that but for Markievicz's financial backing, there would be no Fianna. Even the candles and the oil lamp lighting the hall were supplied by the Countess.[110]

The reaction of *Sinn Féin* was muted, and its report was barely functional:

> … we have received a communication that a National Boys Brigade under the title Fianna Éireann was formed at a meeting in the hall on Monday evening, and that a further meeting, to which boys are invited, will be held there on Friday evening.

Seán Ó Dubghaill, a representative of the local branch of the Sinn Féin party and the Gaelic League, was at pains to disassociate both groups from Na Fianna: they had 'no connection with the affair' and were not 'in any way identified with it'.[111] Sinn Féin, at this point, was a flimsy organisation on the nationalist periphery. An increase in the number of branches from twenty-one in 1906 to 128 in 1909 only served to camouflage the real decline evidenced by its decreasing membership and fiscal shortcomings. In the twelve months prior to August 1909, nearly half of the clubs in Ireland had failed to fulfil any of their financial obligations. Sinn Féin had effectively ceased to exist as an active political force outside of one central branch in Dublin. There were only 581 registered party members, 215 of them in Dublin. Sales of the weekly edition of the *Sinn Féin* newspaper peaked at 64,515 in September 1909, but had dropped to under 30,000 by January 1910. A daily edition appeared for six months, but was abandoned in January 1910.[112]

The transformation of Sinn Féin into the most powerful political machine in the country in the two years after the Rising had its genesis in the split in the Volunteers in September 1914. Following this, Eoin MacNeill's Irish Volunteers were widely referred to as 'Sinn Féin' Volunteers. As far as Inspector-General Colonel Sir Neville Chamberlain of the Royal Irish Constabulary was concerned in July 1915, 'the various groups of extreme Nationalists, who regard Mr

John Redmond [leader of the Irish Parliamentary Party] as a traitor and demand complete National independence, are utterly disloyal and for convenience may be classified as Sinn Féiners.'[113]

The result of the popular and official mindset that lumped the Volunteers, IRB and other Irish-Ireland groups, as well as Sinn Féin, under the label of 'Sinn Féiners' was that the Easter Rising was immediately labelled, erroneously, as 'the Sinn Féin Rising'. Between May and September 1917, over seventy Sinn Féin clubs mushroomed around Limerick alone. They were called after Edward (Ned) Daly, Bishop O'Dwyer, Tom Clarke, Seán Heuston, Seán MacDiarmada and Colbert.[114] The martyrs and heroes of 1916 had entered the nationalist pantheon.

An Claidheamh Soluis took a much more positive position than *Sinn Féin* on Na Fianna. Editor Patrick Pearse was 'glad to hear' of the developments, and gave a more detailed account of proceedings:

> … a provisional committee were appointed. … In addition to drilling, route marching and camping, classes for the teaching of the Irish language and history will be started. The subscription has been fixed at one penny per week, so that no national boy will be debarred from joining. A further meeting will be held at the Hall on Friday evening at 8 o'clock to which all Irish boys are invited.[115]

Colbert's history lessons proved motivational. One lecture focussed on the 'achievements carried out by the members [of the ancient Fianna] – the tests and examinations they had to pass – before being admitted'. Seamus Kavanagh 'found all those things very inspiring. It helped to make me very enthusiastic about the whole movement'.[116] Arrangements were made for outdoor exercises, and scouting activities got under way almost immediately:

> The section known as the 'Red Branch' spent a most enjoyable six days camping on the slopes of the Three Rock Mountain. On Sunday they were joined by the President and some other members, and 'scouting' games were played. The damp evenings were passed quickly with the singing of Irish songs and talks of Irish heroes.[117]

Colbert occasionally led night marches, starting from Camden Street at 11pm:

> From the time we moved off we were confined to strict silence – neither talking nor smoking – halting every hour for a ten minutes' rest. This was a test of our ability to keep silent. Arriving at some part of the Dublin mountains at daybreak, we halted and were allowed to talk and smoke, and lighted fires and prepared our breakfast. Having had our breakfast and rested, we saw to it that all the fires were put out and started on our journey back to the city.[118]

By the end of the year, the advanced nationalist press was taking Na Fianna increasingly seriously:

> There are those who think the organisation of little importance because it is made up of boys, but such people forget that though one may be too young to be the possessor of that powerful weapon called a vote, nobody is too young to serve his country, and, if necessary, fight for his country.[119]

Liam Mellows, writing in 1917, recalled enjoying the atmosphere and demands of Fianna training:

> Every Sunday marches out were held and these were made the occasion of still further fostering a rebel spirit. ... the Dublin Mountains was the goal of the Dublin Boys every Sunday. Rations were brought and cooked, some of the boys developing great skill in the culinary art, while considerable ingenuity was shown in the way fires and cooking places were built and arrangements made for hanging pots and pans over them.

The camping element of these trips was less pleasant, according to Mellows, but its under-resourced and inexpert practitioners, of which Colbert was one, were not expecting instant gratification:

> Want of funds and want of experience were not exactly a combination conducive to success. Nevertheless a few, headed by Con Colbert, heroically suffered all the discom-

forts attendant on camping in the most primitive manner, believing that it was fitting them to fight the good fight later on.

Despite the often trying conditions, spirits apparently remained resolutely high, and uncontaminated by what Mellows considered to be the threat of cultural pollution:

Whether tired on the march or cold at night in camp, scorched by the sun or drenched by the rain, the boys always sung and laughed and joked. And the songs they sang, not the vulgar suggestive inanities from the music halls, vile importations from England that were perhaps the best proof of how far Anglicisation had eaten into the national life of Ireland, were the songs of resurgent Ireland, ballads that breathed patriotism, love of country, rebellion and defiance.[120]

These hikes and route marches were not entirely innocent affairs, designed solely to get city boys out into the fresh air. Rather, they were very deliberate training courses:

… we got to know every field, byroad, every farmhouse where there was running water, the name of the river, how many water pumps and even how many RIC men in each barracks. This was always an observation test and every boy would have his particular task to do, check motorcars, bikes, horse carts, cattle and sheep in fields.[121]

Its cultural emphasis was indisputable, but elements of the Fianna programme – scouting, fieldcraft, and eventually shooting – were unambiguously military.

Colbert was one of the recruiting officers, and his earliest efforts 'attracted much derision'. Many of the first Fianna members, as the sons of Fenian families, did not need much convincing. He also had some success with nationalist school-teachers, who allowed him to talk to their pupils. Brother Carey in Synge Street Catholic Boys' School 'allowed him to explain that it was the first open organisation to work for the independence of Ireland'. The teacher's subsequent warning to his students about the perils of entanglement in secret societies was not heeded in every instance.[122]

Training included first aid, signalling and map reading, as well as the drilling, marching and Irish lessons with which Colbert was heavily involved. Like most of his fellow organisers, Colbert had little experience relevant to scouting. Colbert was the first Fianna instructor in elementary drill formations, but Eamon Martin was 'afraid he was no great expert at this time':

> By intense swotting, however, he improved as the weeks went on, and, consequently, so did the sluagh [branch] … in a comparatively short time we had left the 'form fours' stage behind us, and had advanced to section and company formations, to signalling and all the rest of a fairly comprehensive course.[123]

The use of the Irish language was emphasised, and officers attended a class taught by Patrick Pearse in the Ard Craobh of the Gaelic League. They in turn taught the boys in their respective sluaighte. Colbert prepared a set of Irish-language drill commands for the organisation, which were to become the accepted version. From early 1911, all commands were given in Irish, at least in An Céad Sluagh.[124] The Irish language should probably be considered to have been one of the most powerful tools at the disposal of Na Fianna, providing as it did an expression of internal cohesion, and aiding in the self-definition of identity against external enemies.

As well as An Céad Sluagh at Camden Street, Colbert took charge of Sluagh Emmet, at 10 North Beresford Place. Protestant United Irishman Robert Emmet, who was entering his mid-twenties when he staged the 1803 rebellion, was another youthful figure who Na Fianna were encouraged to look up to and emulate. Colbert lauded him in verse:

Oh! He the martyr of our martyrs
He a hero all our own.
Part of the great resurrecting nation
And of her alone.
Ireland has idol! – his first and last love,
His ambition, his joy, his pride he loved while hope lived in her
And when hope died he died
Murdered by the brutal Saxon
Murdered by a nation's slovenliness.[125]

Sluagh Emmet functioned under the auspices of the North Dock branch of Sinn Féin, which was warming to Na Fianna. Also known as the North Dock Sluagh, Sluagh Emmet had Irish history lectures every Sunday night from a Councillor Gregan, a retired teacher. Sluagh Emmet wore cotton shirts, with green slouch hats and blue shorts.[126] When the Irish Transport and General Workers' Union subsequently bought the building and renamed it Liberty Hall, Na Fianna maintained their presence there.

The first couple of annual Fianna conventions, or Ard Fheiseanna, were held in Markievicz's Surrey House home on Leinster Road in Rathmines. Sydney Gifford – sister of Muriel, who married Thomas MacDonagh, and Grace, who married Joseph Plunkett – described how the house was competely given over to the boys:

> When all available bedrooms had been taken up, rolls of blankets were laid out in the drawing room so that others could bivouac on the floor at night. There were plenty of pipers, dancers, singers, fiddlers and elocutionists among them, and many an impromptu ceilidhe was held in Surrey House when Na Fianna were there in force. Some of the boys, including Liam Mellows, Con Colbert and Eamon Martin wore kilts and this gave a festive air to the gathering.

Gifford could picture Colbert 'standing up to recite some patriotic poem':

He was a powerfully built lad, a little under medium height, with broad shoulders and a finely shaped head. When he spoke, his soft Limerick voice took on a passionate ring, and the expression on his face changed from its usual gentle and dreamy look to one of fierce purpose. As he stood there, holding his body taut and his hands gripped firmly behind his back, he seemed the very personification of a young pikeman of '98.[127]

The Dublin District Council of Na Fianna came into being in the autumn of 1911, and Captain Colbert was elected chairman. By this point the combined Dublin sluaighte were marching every Sunday to Scoil Éanna, Rathfarnham, for field drill.[128] Pearse took a deep interest in the movement, allowing Na Fianna to use the grounds surrounding the school for camping and manoeuvres, and establishing a sluagh among the pupils. As with several other sluaighte, Colbert inspected them regularly, and cycled out from the city to train them once a week. Well before Pearse joined the IRB at the end of 1913, Colbert had no scruples about recruiting some of the Scoil Éanna Fianna sluagh into the Brotherhood without their headmaster's knowledge: There were about six boys involved and, as Desmond Ryan explained, 'as Pearse was not in the I.R.B. at that time he could not understand why we disappeared at certain times'.[129] When Colbert involved IRB trainees in the Scoil Éanna fête in the public ground in Jones' Road (later Croke Park), in order to swell the numbers of the marching formations, the Pearse brothers marvelled innocently at his military genius in raising an army overnight. They apparently regarded Colbert as a Napoleon-like figure. Colbert was unimpressed by their naivety.[130]

The Fianna organisation expanded from the fifteen sluaighte affiliated nationally at the 1911 Ard Fheis to twenty-two in 1912, concentrated in urban areas. If its growth in numbers was not overwhelming, its increase in efficiency was more impressive. That the annual Ard Fheis was by now habitually held in the Oak Room of the Mansion House, Dublin, rather than at Markievicz's home, indicates that Na Fianna had come quite a distance in a short space of time, metaphorically if not literally, from its original 'dingy hall' in Camden Street. Colbert, Seán Heuston and Michael Lonergan were three of the five IRB men elected to the Ard Choisde (the governing body when the Ard Fheis was not sitting).[131]

Colbert had joined the IRB 'at an early stage', according to Marnie Hay.[132] This seems to have been even before the foundation of Na Fianna. Art O'Donnell, Colbert's first cousin and brigadier of the West Clare Volunteers during the War of Independence, recalled Con visiting the family home at Tullycrine and swearing him into the IRB. This was in 1908.[133]

The IRB had been conspiring to achieve Irish independence by force since the 1850s, but for long periods had been riven by internal bickering and decimated by the loss of its leadership to imprisonment and exile. Changes in personnel were now reinvigorating the Brotherhood, however, and radicals like Tom Clarke and Seán MacDiarmada had displaced conservative elements in its Supreme Council by 1910–11. The emergence of Na Fianna presented the IRB with opportunity and means for the military training of its younger members, and its influence spread amongst the Dublin sluaighte.

Hobson assumed the key organisational position of chairman of the IRB Dublin Centres Board in 1912. He prioritised preparations for what he envisioned as a national military volunteer organisation. This involved creating a dedicated Fianna IRB circle, the John Mitchel Literary and Debating Society. Colbert was appointed Centre, and other members included senior Fianna officers Lonergan, Heuston (after he moved from Limerick to Dublin in 1913 to continue his work with the Great Southern and Western Railway Company), Pádraig Ó Riain, Seán McGarry, Liam Mellows and Eamon Martin. They guaranteed a strong link between Na Fianna and the IRB.

The association with the Fianna also ensured a strong representation of Scoil Éanna students in the Mitchel circle.[134] Their duties included enrolling appropriate candidates in the Brotherhood once they reached the age of seventeen. Martin, for instance, recruited Liam Mellows to the IRB, and Colbert swore him in.[135] Colbert was as enthusiastic about this responsibility as all his others. When on holidays in Athea in 1913, he suggested to Éamon Dore, Ned Daly's brother-in-law, that he join the Brotherhood, not knowing he was already a member.[136]

Some simply did not submit to the allure of Fenianism. Martin and Colbert requested the allegiance of Seamus Pounch, but he refused 'on conscientious grounds', objecting to the secret nature of the society. Pounch was satisfied that his 'attitude was understood'.[137] Nonetheless, Martin claimed that by 1913, practically every senior Fianna officer throughout the country had become a member of the IRB.[138] For Patrick Ward, another of Colbert's recruits, the connection was so strong that he went so far as to state, 'the Fianna had originally been started with the definite purpose of recruiting young blood for the IRB'.[139]

Clandestine training was carried out in various halls, but principally in the Irish National Foresters' Hall, 41 Parnell Square (where Pádraig Ó Riain's father worked as caretaker).[140] The hall was also known as the North City Gymnasium Club.[141] From 1912, training included instruction in small arms.[142] Colbert and the others acquired most of their knowledge from British army manuals, and culled from them liberally, issuing stencilled copies to the company and section leaders of each sluagh.[143] As both a recruiter and a trainer, then, Colbert played a pivotal role in revitalising the IRB.

This paid dividends in the summer of 1913 – when Hobson proposed to the IRB hierarchy that a militia should be established, he was able to provide readymade officers from Na Fianna. It was in bridging the transition between cultural revival, separatist conspiracy and public declaration of force in the form of the Volunteers, and in further radicalising a corps of already ardently nationalist boys, that Na Fianna played its most important role.

Chapter 4
• • • • •

The Volunteers

T he Home Rule Bill of 1886 did not pass the House of Commons at Westminster. The 1893 Bill made it through the Commons, but was vetoed by the House of Lords. Unionists, particularly in Ulster, mounted mass opposition on each occasion. They would go further in the years before the Rising. From 1906, the Liberal party dominated the Commons, but their policies were often stymied by the Conservative-controlled House of Lords. When the Chancellor for the Exchequer, David Lloyd George, attempted to finance both social reforms and the arms race against Germany with increased taxes in 1909, the Lords took the unprecedented step of rebuffing the budget.

Two general elections in 1910 left John Redmond's Irish Party holding the balance of power in parliament. He traded votes to Herbert Asquith's Liberals in return for the promise of a third Home Rule Bill. The permanent stumbling block of the Lord's veto was reduced to a temporary

Charcoal sketch of Con Colbert by Seán O'Sullivan, circa 1941.

Left: Commemorative poster of Colbert by O'Loughlin, Murphy & Boland Ltd., Dublin, 1917.

Below: Colbert's Pioneer Total Abstinence League of the Sacred Heart pledge form, dated 31 December 1906.

Lucy Smyth, 'the nicest girl in Dublin', and, inset, her Cumann na mBan first aid certificate.

Above: A drilling lesson in Scoil Éanna's 'gymnasium'. Note the kilts and the school crest adorning the boys' jumpers, as well as the accompanying piper.

Below: Na Fianna Éireann Ard Fheis, Mansion House, Dublin, circa 1912. In the centre of the second row from the front, we see Liam Mellows, Countess Markievicz, Pádraig Ó Riain and Con Colbert.

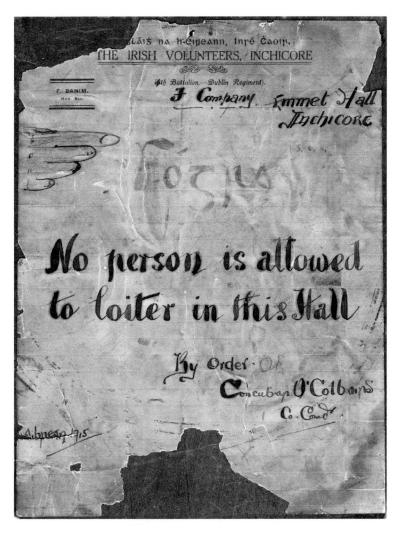

Fógra: a notice from the wall of Emmet Hall, Inchicore,
signed by Colbert.

Above: A Na Fianna Éireann 'physical culture class' at their hall in Barrington Street, Limerick, 1913.

Below: Na Fianna council. Front row, left to right: Paddy Holahan, Michael Lonergan, Con Colbert. Back row: Gary Holahan, Pádraig Ó Riain.

Above: At the rear of Na Fianna Hall, Barrington Street, Limerick, circa 1913. Standing, left to right: Joe Halpin, Joe Dalton, unidentified, perhaps Con Colbert holding the flag (although it is impossible to be sure given that his face is obscured and the possibly distorted perception of height), Seán Heuston, Jack Dalton, Ned Fitzgibbon. Seated, left to right: Patrick Whelan, John Daly, James Leddin.
Below: 'The Revolt of Sinn Féiners in Ireland.' 'Sinn Féiners' parading.

Jameson's distillery, Marrowbone Lane. This photograph gives a sense of how vast the site was. However, its position on the edge of the city meant its influence on the development of the Rising was peripheral.

delaying power by the Parliament Act of 1911.

Unionists reacted with great fury, effectively imposing their own embargo. There were 891,000 Protestants in Ulster in 1911 to 691,000 Catholics. The 250,000 Protestants in the three other provinces made up only ten percent of the population. Even before the Bill was introduced, Ulster unionists, determined to preserve their distinct identity in a distinct state, were explicit in their resolve to embrace illegality if necessary to evade Home Rule.

Like its incarnations of 1886 and 1893, the Bill brought before the Commons in April 1912 proposed nothing so extreme as a republic. It might be hyperbole to describe it as not offering much more than a glorified form of local government, but under the Bill Westminster would retain control of basic necessities of sovereignty such as defence and foreign policy, trade and even policing. Unionists had genuine convictions that Home Rule would, in the words of Ulster's Solemn League and Covenant,

> be disastrous to the material well-being of Ulster as well as
> of the whole of Ireland, subversive of our civil and religious
> freedom, destructive of our citizenship and perilous to the
> unity of the Empire.

Some of the terms of the Covenant, which referred to 'defeating the present conspiracy to set up a Home Rule Parliament in Ireland', were profoundly anti-democratic and anti-liberal. As many as 400,000 men and 250,000 women signed pledges to the effect that they would stand together in refuting Home Rule by any means. The interplay of issues of class, privilege, race and religion created ambivalence regarding the proper treatment of the potential minority. The most vociferous may have regarded Catholics as a lesser breed, their intellectual and moral inferiors, and assumed that nationalists would automatically establish a replica ascendancy.[144] If this was an ill-founded anxiety, the risk of Home Rule equating to 'Rome Rule' had more substance.

The loyalism of unionists ultimately proved not to be to the Crown, but to Ulster Protestantism. The same democratic contradictions were inherent in the advanced nationalist position on self-determination, as they were in the Allies' rhetoric on this theme in Europe between 1914 and 1918. Those most insistent on applying their own prerogative in Ireland while rejecting unionist objections claimed unconditional jurisdiction over a million mostly non-Catholic and non-Gaelic people. Colbert addressed the topic only briefly and at a rather superficial level. His thoughts from 1909 on 'Orangemen and the Nation' were that 'English intrigue' had caused and maintained discontent between Catholic and Protestant, and 'made it a war of Catholic South against Orange North'.[145]

The Orange Order had taken the lead in drilling and arming men since 1911 and, against a backdrop of progressively hardline unionist rhetoric, the Ulster Volunteer Force came into being in early 1913. The gunmen were stepping out of the shadows, prompting Patrick Pearse to observe in late 1913 that 'I think the Orangeman with a rifle a much less ridiculous figure than a nationalist without a rifle'.[146] The Irish Volunteers were founded on 25 November 1913 in Dublin. Bulmer Hobson, on behalf of the IRB, was heavily involved in engineering its establishment, but the immediate catalyst was Eoin MacNeill's article in *An Claidheamh Soluis*, 'The North began', which called on nationalists to arm themselves in defence of Home Rule as unionists had done in opposition.

Colbert joined the Irish Volunteers at their inception, and was among half-a-dozen Fianna (Hobson, Ó Riain, Martin, Lonergan and Liam Mellows were the others)[147] and more than a dozen IRB activists elected to the thirty-one-member provisional committee. There were also eight Home Rulers and four Sinn Féiners on this executive. Patrick Pearse, Joseph Plunkett and Thomas MacDonagh were initially unaligned, but would subsequently commit to and reinforce Fenian influence behind the scenes.[148] John Redmond, conscious of the IRB element and harbouring reservations about the potential of such a movement to undermine his authority, was hesitant to offer support. The rapid increase in Volunteer membership in the spring and early summer of 1914 to more than 150,000 forced his hand, however. The Inspector-General of the Royal Irish Constabulary pointed out that:

Each county will soon have a trained army far outnumber-
ing the police, and those who control the Volunteers will be
in a position to dictate to what extent the law of the land
may be carried into effect.[149]

But the majority were determined to fulfil the Home Rule
Bill, which had just passed through the House of Commons,
rather than destroy it.

The startling expansion in the numbers of Irish Volunteers
was again a reaction to events in the north of the country.
British double standards surrounding the Ulster Volunteers
were exposed by the so-called 'Curragh mutiny' in March,
which illustrated that the officer class in the army would
not support any government moves to quash unionist resistance to Home Rule, while the Larne gun-running in May,
involving the illegal importation of 25,000 German rifles,
was overlooked by the authorities. There would be a mark-
edly different reaction to the Irish Volunteers' Howth gun-
running in July.

The upshot was that Redmond had to abandon his oppo-
sition to the nationalist militia. Instead, having criticised
the provisional committee as non-representative, in June he
issued the ultimatum that twenty-five members of the Irish
Party be co-opted. The committee met in what one member,
Seán Fitzgibbon, reservedly termed 'a strained atmosphere'.
Thomas MacDonagh, busy supervising a centre for the
Intermediate Examinations, which were underway at the

time, was the only absentee. He did, however, send a letter expressing his opposition to the proposal. MacNeill presided, and reluctantly proposed the admission of Redmond's nominees. Colonel Maurice Moore, the military director of the Volunteers, Roger Casement and Hobson followed suit.[150]

In fact, the majority of the members of the provisional committee, swayed by the appeal to comply in order to avoid a split in the organisation, acceded to Redmond's demand. Hobson hoped that the IRB could maintain its control, and while a split was postponed until after the outbreak of the war in Europe, Tom Clarke and Seán MacDiarmada, the most powerful members of the IRB executive, had lost faith in him.

Colbert was one of only nine of the Volunteer executive who opposed the measure, notwithstanding the great pressure brought to bear on him by Bulmer Hobson and his coterie. The other eight were Éamonn Ceannt, Michael Judge, Seán Fitzgibbon, Eamon Martin, Patrick Pearse, Seán MacDiarmada, and Piaras Beaslai. Fitzgibbon and Judge were the only non-IRB members. Appealing to the Volunteers to hold fast, the nine dissenters explained the grounds of their opposition:

> … it was a violation of the basic principles which up to
> the present have carried the Volunteers to success, [but] at
> the same time feel it our duty to continue our work in the
> movement; and we appeal to those of the rank and file who

are in agreement with us on this point to sink their personal feelings and persist in their efforts to make the Irish Volunteers an efficient armed National Defence Force.[151]

If there had been a possibility that whatever revolutionary enterprise emerged would not be a minority undertaking, it was scuppered in this moment. The protagonists of the Rising moved in ever decreasing circles of trust.

One political development that accompanied the eruption of war in August and that would have significant repercussions for republicans for several years was the inauguration of the draconian Defence of the Realm Act (DORA). Martial law was routinely invoked in British colonies in times of crisis (such as in Ireland in 1798), but had not been instituted at home for centuries, and would have been a last resort even in the event of invasion or other unspecified military emergency. Instead, parliament passed DORA, which allowed for courts martial of civilians suspected of contravening any of its mass of regulations. This would prove particularly important in the aftermath of the Rising.

DORA was updated and implemented at regular intervals until the end of the War of Independence in 1921. It was the principal legal measure designed to suppress political dissent, and was used to curb the freedom of the press, freedom of speech, and the conduct of public meetings. Republicans were arrested, imprisoned and deported without recourse to civil law. At different points, newspapers were shut down, organisations like the Gaelic League and the GAA were banned, and social gatherings such as fairs were prohibited.

The Irish Party appeared to be in an unassailable position as the government-in-waiting before Home Rule was side-lined by the war. It would never be implemented. Redmond followed imperial policy and, in September, called on members of the Volunteers to join the British army. The movement was sundered apart, as all advanced nationalists, most of whom had acquiesced in June, now felt compelled to repudiate him. The vast majority, however, remained under the Redmondite banner, and became known as the National Volunteers. Like the Ulster Volunteers, many of them subsequently enlisted in the army. The minority, under Eoin Mac-Neill, retained the title of Irish Volunteers.

Redmond's support for the war ultimately undermined both the Irish Party and his Volunteers. The ostensible achievement of Home Rule had boosted his prestige and created goodwill towards Britain, but Redmond's stock fell and the store of goodwill dissipated as the war progressed. As fear generated by the threat of conscription became more pressing, the identification of the Irish Party with recruiting was a critical factor in its loss of support.

The party was not strong enough to respond effectively to the crisis generated by the Rising. In this context, Sinn Féin thrived, as it appealed to the anti-recruiting sentiments of the majority of nationalists. Redmond was a prisoner of

circumstances beyond his control. The war, rather than unit-
ing nationalists and unionists, drove a further wedge between
them, and also accentuated the divisions within nationalism.
Nevertheless, a more resolute leader than Redmond could
possibly have won more concessions from the Liberals as
a price for his support. If this had happened, the apparent
inevitability of a republican war of separation may not have
materialised.

The fact that a large majority chose to follow Redmond
distorts the degree of enthusiasm with which his endorse-
ment of the war effort was greeted. The National Volunteers
showed little immediate desire to join the army. Attendances
at drilling exercises declined substantially. This was partly due
to a lack of competent instructors who, as reservists, were
called to the colours. However, the principal factor was not
the absence of political necessity since the passing of Home
Rule, but rather that men believed they would be required
to join the army if they continued to parade. There was also
an element of discontent among members of the National
Volunteers, who were dissatisfied with the foisting of ex-
officers with strong unionist views on them by the central
leadership in Dublin.[152]

The Rising should also be interpreted as an anti-war statement. James Connolly, defending himself at his court-martial, was very clear that the rebels were taking a stand against
the war:

We went out to break the connection between this country
and the British Empire and to establish an Irish Republic.
We believe that the call we thus issued to the people of Ireland was a nobler call in a holier cause than any call issued
to them during this war having any connection with the
war. We succeeded in proving that Irishmen are ready to die
endeavouring to win for Ireland their national rights which
the British Government has been asking them to die to win
for Belgium.[153]

The socially conservative Redmond, like his predecessor
Parnell, was not shy of flirting with violent disorder when
he felt such a recipe would benefit his political agenda and
the circumstances were under his control. Despite his pro-
pensity for political compromise and concession, Redmond
had not hesitated to harness potentially revolutionary unrest
in his efforts to achieve legislative reform. He had manipu-
lated social discontent over agrarian issues in earlier years,
and infiltrated the Volunteers.

The means and ends of constitutional and physical-force
nationalism often closely coincided. Constitutional nationalism and violent agrarian agitation, for instance, had intersected at various points for several decades before the Rising.
William Lundon, an ex-Fenian who was MP for East Limerick, explained in 1904 that his understanding of Home Rule
did not mean

... a little parliament in Dublin that would pay homage to the big one, but a sovereign and independent one and if he had his own way he would break the remaining links that bound the two countries ... he was trained in another school in '67 (loud cheers) and he was not a parliamentarian when he walked with his rifle on his shoulder on the night of the 5th of March (cheers).

Lundon's remarks exemplify the type of oratory which lent the popular rhetoric of the IPP a vigorous Faith and Fatherland character. Pro-imperial attitudes identifying an Anglicised, secularised Home Rule Ireland were the preserve of a minority. Such evocations as Lundon's, in combination with the mirage-like, abstract quality of Home Rule and regular references to the historic cause and struggle of the Irish nation, created a more advanced popular image of the Parliamentary Party than would otherwise have been the case. Coupled with the credit it claimed for ameliorative British social and democratic legislation, the populist patriotism of the Parliamentary Party secured its grip on the hearts and minds of majority nationalist support.[154]

The apparently rapid conversion of public opinion after the Rising might be better understood if the constitutional and physical-force traditions were not seen as mutually exclusive. When 'The Soldiers' Song' (Amhrán na bhFiann) supplanted 'God Save Ireland' as the emblematic tune of nationalist Ireland after 1916, it signified not a transformation but a hardening of attitudes. The ultimate aim remained the same, but there was a wider diffusion of support for more militant methods in its pursuit. Patrick Pearse, shortly after the foundation of the Volunteers and around the time he was sworn into the IRB, was determined to win over the hearts and minds of constitutionalists. He told John Daly that he wished

> ... to find a response in the Home Rule heart as well as in the Nationalist heart, more properly so called. I believe that the rank and file of the Home Rulers are ready, if properly handled, to go as far as you have gone and I hope to go. Here again the Volunteer movement seems to be the one thing that will bring them into line with us.[155]

This is a prime example of what Desmond Ryan referred to as Pearse's 'extraordinary outlook on insurrection in which he believed so strongly that he persuaded himself that everyone must at heart agree with him'.[156]

On the ground, Colbert was one of the first drill instructors, and was involved in the selection and training of officers, just as he had been in Na Fianna. Most of the new Volunteer officers were IRB men who had been trained by senior Fianna members. Na Fianna also flooded the rank and file of the Volunteers, by introducing a new practice whereby members who had reached the age of eighteen and had limited opportunity for progression through the ranks were automatically transferred to the Volunteers:

> It gave to the Volunteers [eighteen-year-olds] who were
> already fully trained and for the Fianna it solved the prob-
> lem of the young men of eighteen years and over, for whom
> there were not sufficient officer positions.[157]

And while co-operation between the two organisations
was always close, Hobson pointed out that 'at no time prior
to the Rising was there any formal affiliation'.[158]

Colbert was quickly appointed captain of F Company, 4th
Battalion, Dublin Brigade, a rank which he held until the
Rising. Many of the Volunteers under his command were
Fianna graduates. F Company was based in Inchicore, a British garrison district, and like so many Volunteer units around
the country, was initally instructed by British army reservists.
Their route marches took them from Inchicore to the Magazine and around the Phoenix Park.[159] Much of Colbert's Volunteer activity was centred on Emmet Hall workmen's club,
the premises of the Inchicore branch of the Irish Transport
and General Workers' Union. Adjacent to Richmond army
barracks, it was home to Michael Mallin, who led the Irish
Citizen Army with James Connolly. Colbert's section of the
Volunteers would often engage in mock attacks against the
Citizen Army. As well as being valuable teaching exercises,
these engagements helped to develop a sense of camaraderie between the Volunteers and Citizen Army which did not
always exist elsewhere.[160] There was a plot of ground at the
back of the workmen's club for drilling.[161]

The strength of F Company before the Redmondite split was estimated at 800 by three members, and 600 by another.[162] Appraisals of the number which remained immediately thereafter varied from fifteen to fifty, and while the figure on paper rose substantially again by the spring of 1916, to perhaps as many as 200, it is reasonably certain that no more than thirty-six turned out on Easter Monday.[163] The minority who originally continued under Colbert came from just a few families. They included the O'Neills, Powers, Carthys and Troys, who were all related to each other.[164]

Each company in the Dublin Brigade was organised in four sections, and each section consisted of two squads, formed on a residential basis in such a manner as to facilitate rapid mobilisation. Sections 1 and 2 were in the charge of a First Lieutenant, and sections 3 and 4 were in the charge of a Second Lieutenant. Each squad was in the charge of a Squad-Commander. Colbert's Lieutenants in F Company were Christy Byrne and Larry Murtagh. His Quartermaster was Peadar Doyle. His section leaders included Tom Young, Edward O'Neill and Liam Power.

Colbert was interested in the psychology of leadership. Since the Volunteers did not have a legally enforceable code of discipline or detention akin to a regular army, an alternative mechanism was necessary. Colbert's approach was to rely on the establishment and maintenance of mutual respect among the group. Motivation by ideal and leadership by example were crucial:

> If a leader is to keep his position, he must act impartially
> towards everyone in his section, he must be on good terms
> with his section, he must show those whom he leads that
> he is capable of leading them and make them clearly under-
> stand he expects them to be respected ... every leader must
> be ideal if his section is to approach anything like perfec-
> tion. Be respectful to your colonel and your men will treat
> you with respect ... Now in regard to most things a man's
> word must be taken as absolute truth. If a member kicks up
> a row and says he did not do so, believe him. In this way,
> every member will get accustomed to be relied on.[165]

Despite the attractiveness of Colbert's theories, it is not surprising that the majority of F Company men had trans- ferred their allegiance to Redmond's National Volunteers. Much of the local Inchicore population had direct ties to the military, or were at least somewhat economically depend- ent on it. There would be a hostile reaction in the area to the surrendered rebels after the Rising as they were escorted through the streets to Richmond barracks.

The sheer density of interconnections between Britain and Ireland by the eve of the war was most powerfully expressed in the mass volunteering of Irishmen (a majority of whom were Catholic) for service in the British army, for a variety of reasons. The British-Irish link was then further cemented in the blood-sacrifice of the trenches. But this must be set in the context of available propaganda resources, the collective communal pressures involved in working-class recruitment, and the financial benefits on offer. Some companies offered workers incentives to join the army and promised to keep their positions open. Economic concerns were a crucial factor for prospective members of the MacNeillite Volunteers also. In April 1915, the organisation formed an insurance society, An Cumann Cosanta, to protect members 'against victimisation, the possibility of which we have learned through experience'.[166] The persecution they were most likely to face because of their political activities was loss of employment.[167] Volunteers explained that

> Employers at the time wielded a most potent weapon … the weapon of economic pressure, or to use a cruder phrase, the threat of starvation … a married man with a family, was confronted with the blunt choice, 'The Volunteers or your job'. Who could blame him for choosing his job?

It was 'tantamount to leaving a job to join, because the employers, in the main, were bitterly opposed to the Irish Volunteers'; 'employees of a considerable number of business concerns were told that they must desist parading with the "Sinn Féin" section of the Volunteers or lose their employment'.[168]

In looking at why individuals joined the Volunteers, it is important to stress the significance of social and collective influences. Romantic patriotism and youthful camaraderie were factors, but there was a communal element also, often involving friends and relatives. Having an active family member could be decisive. Local bonds held companies together. The ranks of F Company consisted of 'practically a few families of brothers'.[169] None of this is to dismiss the strength of ideological commitment as a determining dynamic within the republican cause, but traditions of political activism within families and the influence of family members were paramount in the entry of young men and women into the militant movement.[170]

Volunteering was not merely a social gathering of like-minded young men. It represented an organised resolve to confront the British presence in Ireland by means of force. The elimination of destablising and demoralising political rivalries after the split provided the Irish Volunteers with a new unity of purpose and made them a more cohesive military unit. Redmond's influence had been removed and this suited the IRB. However, the continuing presence of IRB agents within the Volunteers meant that divisions remained, particularly among the leadership. These divisions were most profoundly manifested in the intrigues and uncertainties of Easter week 1916.

As IRB influence grew within Na Fianna, its rhetoric

became increasingly confrontational. Colbert may initially have been recruiting Pearse's students surreptitiously, but by 1914 they were of one mind. Pearse recognised the value of the militant mentality fostered in Na Fianna:

> We believe that Na Fianna Éireann have kept the military spirit alive in Ireland during the past four years, and that if the Fianna had not been founded in 1909, the Volunteers of 1913 would never have arisen. In a sense, then, the Fianna have been the pioneers of the Volunteers; and it is from the ranks of the Fianna that the Volunteers must be recruited.[171]

As Marnie Hay pointed out, this reasoning could be extended to draw a direct line of continuity from the foundation of Na Fianna in 1909 to the Rising in 1916.[172] Pearse further declared that 'the object of Na Fianna Éireann is to train the boys of Ireland to fight Ireland's battles when they are men':

> … we hope to train Irish boys from their earliest years to be soldiers, not only to know the trade of a soldier – drilling, marching, camping, signalling, scouting, and (when they are old enough) shooting – but also, what is far more important, to understand and prize military discipline and to have a military spirit.[173]

Helena Molony commented that 'the boys loved playing at soldiers', but if there was any suggestion that Na Fianna was merely indulging innocuous fantasy, any doubt as to its deadly intent and the fact that it was preparing boys to kill and be killed, its progressively militant trajectory clearly indicated otherwise.[174] Colbert was ruthless in this regard. Drilling and handling arms were the practical applications of the idealisation of the ancient Fianna warriors. Many members eventually proved that they were willing to follow this through to its logical conclusion. For Gary Holohan, who inflicted one of the first fatalities of the Rising, his 'outlook on life was completely changed':

> The Fianna was no longer a mere pastime or social function. It became a sacred duty, and I started to bend my every effort towards the freeing of Ireland. No task was too great or time too long.

Holohan remembered 'getting a real gun in my hands for the first time while on sentry duty [at Markievicz's Belcamp House in Raheny]. It was a great sensation'.[175]

Although one Fianna member places him at the scene, it seem that Colbert did not participate when the Volunteers, assisted by Na Fianna, put into practice some of the skills they had been learning in training, bringing ashore hundreds of rifles smuggled from Germany by Erskine Childers at Howth on 26 July 1914. Colbert, ignorant of the plans, was more likely in Killarney at the summer school of the Oireachtas, the annual Irish culture, music and language festival.[176]

The gun-running was a success for the Volunteers on several levels. Firstly, it exposed the fragility of Redmond's control. More importantly perhaps, it was a public relations coup. Not only did it happen in broad daylight near the capital, but the response of the State was diametrically opposed to the inaction at Larne a month earlier. Police unsuccessfully attempted to disarm the Volunteers, while the army fired on a crowd and killed three civilians in the city centre later in the day. Colbert's absence illustrates that he was at a remove from the centre of decision-making and power.

The Dublin Fianna began to train with Howth rifles shortly thereafter. The first place they tried them was in the garden of Surrey House, home of Markievicz: 'we satisfied ourselves of its deadly accuracy. But, owing to the big explosion, we had to desist as the quiet neighbourhood of Rathmines was getting excited at the big bangs'. They tried out smaller rifles at 7 Clifton Terrace, the residence of Colbert, where they 'did not attract so much attention as the explosions were not so big'.[177]

Outside of Dublin, it was in Limerick city that Na Fianna made the most pronounced progress. Veteran Fenian John Daly, uncle of Ned Daly, was heavily involved in the formation of the Lord Edward Fitzgerald Sluagh of Na Fianna in Limerick in the summer of 1911, and in its subsequent maintenance. He built a hall for Na Fianna, at the back of his own property on Barrington Street and, in December 1912, presided over the opening ceremonies. Tom Clarke wrote to him that

> ... tis grand to find that you have made the Fianna such a success in Limerick – you are away ahead of anything else in the country – in Dublin they haven't yet gone the length of even thinking about building a hall.[178]

The Lord Edward Fitzgerald Sluagh was the only branch in the country sufficiently well organised to elicit a specific response from the police. From May 1912, when he reported that 210 boys paraded in the city, the Inspector-General of the Royal Irish Constabulary regularly noted that Limerick was the only place where Na Fianna were making any significant progress.[179] Seán Hueston led the Limerick Fianna until he was transferred to Dublin by his employer in 1913. He had up to 250 boys in his charge.[180]

Colbert would regularly visit John Daly in Barrington Street, when passing through Limerick city on his way home to Athea. Madge Daly described the 'deep friendship' that developed between them:

> Con's visits were a source of great pleasure to my uncle as he brought him the latest news of the Fianna, the Wolfe Tone clubs and the other national groups in Dublin. He wrote to him, too, whenever there was a little news.[181]

In August 1913, for instance, Colbert wrote to Daly about developments around Three Rock and Bornaculla in Dublin:

> The Fianna have already started a slua in the district with about a roll of 40 boys, who spend their evenings at drill and signalling, and march then around the roads singing rebel songs, and generally making up their minds to give the Saxon a hot time soon. They will too with God's help. This is part of O'Dwyers's country, you know, and has a good spirit still.[182]

Colbert was publicly chastised by Hobson's acolyte Pádraig Ó Riain, via the *Irish Volunteer* of 13 February 1915. Ó Riain

> … was rather surprised to find that the Left half of [Fianna] Company B, Inchicore, has practically gone out of business. Capt. Colbert, of Company B, is also the local commander of Irish Volunteers. That's all.

This was designed as a less than subtle accusation of neglect against Colbert – that he had abandoned his Fianna slua in favour of the Volunteers. It is true that Colbert concentrated primarily on his Volunteer duties from their foundation, but Ó Riain's gibe could have been motivated by tension between Colbert and Hobson. It ignored the fact that Colbert had delegated his duties in Inchicore to Bob Holland. It also ignored the impact of the Redmondite split on Fianna as well as Volunteer membership, and perhaps failed to realise this was an important stage in the process of radicalisation of the Volunteers, as it was only the more dedicated activists who remained committed to the organisation. Moreover, despite the decline described by Ó Riain, Colbert was still bringing his Fianna company out on camps, as one tired scout described in the *Fianna* of March 1915:

> Dreary winds are howling round us,
> And the tent is shaking o'er us.
> Aching backs and frozen feet;
> Under canvas it's not sweet.
> Fianna's name up we are keeping;
> None of us from cold are sleeping;
> Dawn is coming, we will eat,
> Then for home, for it is sweet.
> Still we cheer our Captain Colbert,
> Who 'roughs it' just the same as we.
> Who can daunt us, what can turn us?
> Homeward boys of Company B.

Ó Riain's barbed comments had no impact on Colbert's standing among the nationalist leadership. Just a week after they were published, Thomas MacDonagh announced an eight-week course of intensve physical training, including forced marches, for the Dublin Brigade. Colbert was to lead the 3rd Battalion in exercises for a fortnight and he was to take the 2nd Battalion for another fortnight. A programme of

Saturday night lectures for officers at HQ was drawn up by the Dublin City and County Board. The third and fourth sessions, by Liam Mellows and Éamon de Valera, were to cover scouting, map reading and map drawing. Colbert would be on hand to provide 'additional notes and illustrations'.[183]

The physical commitment and endurance demanded of Volunteers is evident from accounts of the manoeuvres held over the Easter weekend in 1915. Each company of the Dublin Brigade was requested to make five members available, and 120 men assembled at Rathfarnham. They were under the command of Colbert, Seán Heuston and Liam Clarke:

We set out at 5.30 p.m. on Easter Saturday, 1915. We marched up the Featherbed Mountain to Glencree Reformatory where we had tea in the Gym. The good Brothers warned us to be quiet for fear of distracting the boys. We left the school at about 10.30 p.m. and proceeded via Kippure to the Sally Gap and arrived at a small wood three miles from Rathdrum at 5 a.m. on Easter Sunday morning. We bivouaced in this wood until 9 a.m. and we had a wash up and breakfast and proceeded to Rathdrum for mass. After Mass we were given the remainder of the day off and found a field where we could relax, sleep, cook or anything we had a fancy to do. We fell in at 7 p.m. and marched to Kilcoole where we again bivouaced, i.e. what was left of us as some had gone home by train from Rathdrum. Early next morning before breakfast we moved on to the Glen of the Downs where we breakfasted and rested before setting out on the final stage of our journey to the city which we reached about 6 o'clock on Easter Monday evening.[184]

The *Irish Volunteer* of 17 April 1915 reported that Seán Heuston was organising a Fianna expedition to accompany the Dublin Volunteers on a parade to be held in Limerick on Whitsunday, 23 May. The *National Volunteer* of 29 May described this as a 'Sinn Féin invasion' of Limerick, as Irish Volunteer companies from Dublin, Cork and Tipperary joined their Limerick colleagues to parade through the city.

According to the Dublin Special Branch, about 430 Volunteers, under the command of Patrick Pearse, travelled by train from Dublin that morning, although the figure may well have been nearer 600 when the Fianna contingent was taken into account. The Cork men were in the charge of Terence MacSwiney and Tomás MacCurtain. Tom Clarke, Ned Daly, Seán MacDiarmada, Con Collins, Liam Mellows, Bulmer Hobson and Con Colbert were also in attendance. In total, between 1,100 and 1,200 of what the *Limerick Leader* labelled as 'pro-German' Volunteers marched.

Captain Robert Monteith led the parade. Monteith, a Protestant, had long service, including war experience, in the British army. He was dismissed from his post in the Ordnance Survey and deported from Dublin under DORA in November 1914 for his Volunteer activities. The Volunteer

Executive ordered him to Limerick, where he acted as an organiser and instructor throughout the city and county. In August 1915, at the request of Tom Clarke, Monteith left Limerick and made his way to Germany, via America, where he was to act as drill instructor to Roger Casement's Irish Brigade. He returned from Germany with Casement in Easter week 1916, but the circumstances they met at Banna Strand and beyond meant that he could not contribute anything more to the Rising.[185]

The police estimated that 700 of the Volunteers in Limerick on Whitsunday were armed and had a plentiful supply of ammunition. Between 220 and 250 Fianna members accompanied the Volunteers.[186] The event started off placidly enough:

As we were going down Barrington Street [near the train station] we got the command 'Eyes Right'. The salute was acknowledged by a venerable old man sitting near a window. He looked a huge man and had a long beard. There was a quiet smile on his face. It was John Daly, the Fenian.[187]

The organised, persistent and extensive barracking and physical challenges that they encountered in the Irishtown district in particular, where many people had men-folk serving in the British army, highlighted one section of public opinion at the time. A county Limerick Volunteer recalled that:

We got an awful hiding in Limerick that day, from the mob of the city, who used bottles, bricks and stones, and pots full of urine … pieces of scrap metal and iron bars and knocked many of our lads unconscious, as we marched through Irishtown … However, we did not panic or break ranks but pushed on.[188]

Bob Holland's memories of the 'very hot reception' waiting for them in Irishtown were similar: 'we were pelted with every kind of rubbish, including pots, pans, bottles and jam jars'. It was only after the fact that 'we were warned [by the Volunteer officers] to keep out of certain districts as Limerick at that time was very much a British garrison town'. Holland

… left Limerick with a very bad impression of it and remarked to Con Colbert, who was a Limerick man, that the people of Limerick ought to dispose of their Treaty Stone. Colbert replied that there were bad sheep in every flock.[189]

Dan Breen, who marched with the Tipperary column, wrote that 'we were sorely tempted to open fire on the hostile crowd that pelted us with garbage'.[190] Any such incidence would surely have precipitated a clampdown on the Volunteers and dealt an irrevocable blow to the IRB's ambitions.

Madge Daly, among others, claimed that, some days prior to Whitsunday, a representative of the Redmondite Ancient

Order of Hibernians had come from the headquarters of that organisation in Dublin to foment opposition to the Volunteer parade. Money had been left in all the public houses in the poorer quarters of the city, such as Irishtown, where the separation allowance families lived.[191] Whether or not this was the case, these 'separation wives', who received an allowance in compensation for the absence of their soldier husbands and who feared the potential threat to their livelihoods posed by the Volunteers, would most likely have protested all the same. The separation allowance, however, was viewed in some quarters as a system which facilitated, if not encouraged, excessive consumption of alcohol. A number of soldiers' wives were brought before the City Petty Sessions in September 1915, and it was claimed that '... something should be done to put an end to the drinking habits prevalent among these women ... which, to say the least, constituted a grave scandal'. One magistrate proposed that some form of supervision be imposed on soldiers' wives in receipt of separation allowance, so as to direct their spending.[192]

A local city Volunteer stated that the violence was the work of 'an organised gang of hooligans, all members of the National Volunteers'.[193] A company of County Limerick Volunteers discharged shots into the air at one stage, and fifty police and a number of priests were required to restore order.[194] It was the influence of a priest from the Limerick Arch-Confraternity, rather than the police, that was decisive in restoring calm. Despite the fact that the only consolation that the Volunteers could possibly have taken from the day's events was that they had maintained their discipline in the face of formidable provocation, the following week Pearse wrote, rather sanguinely, to Madge Daly:

> I hope our visit has helped the Limerick Company. We all felt that the great bulk of the people in the city were sympathetic and that the hostile element was small, though noisy. Personally, I found the whole experience useful.[195]

It also seemed to galvanise Colbert's F Company:

> From then on we settled down to more intensive training and drilling. The policy of field work and manoeuvres, although carried out in a small way, gradually gave way to special services such as engineering, the handling of explosives, first aid, signalling, bomb throwing and instructions on street-fighting.[196]

While the debacle over the Volunteer Provisional Committee a year earlier did not diminish Hobson's role within Na Fianna, because his 'counsel and guidance ... so impressed and influenced the young men ... all of whom held him in high esteem', he was no longer trusted by many in the IRB.[197] 'Strange to say', recalled Gary Holohan, the Fianna officers, with the exception of Colbert, 'still had implicit faith' in Hobson, while they in turn enjoyed the full confidence of Tom Clarke and Seán MacDiarmada.[198] Amidst all the intrigue and the complex web of loyalties linking Na Fianna, the Volunteers and the IRB, Colbert's primary allegiance was to the Brotherhood. Hobson retained his control of Na Fianna through the John Mitchel Circle, which had expanded through a drive for recruitment.

The sixth annual Fianna Ard Fheis was held in the Mansion House on Sunday, 11 July 1915. The question of arming Na Fianna arose. Neil MacNeil of E Company (Ranelagh), the son of Eoin MacNeill, proposed a resolution:

> That Fianna adopt as part of the equipment of all third class scouts a Rifle (.22) similar to that of the American Boy Scouts, and that a musketry test be incorporated in the Fianna tests henceforth.

It was carried unanimously.[199]

There was much more dissent when it came to the restructuring of Na Fianna's government. Eamon Martin proposed the dissolution of the Fianna presidency and its replacement by a chief scout, who would assume military command of the organisation. He further suggested that the *ard-choisde* should be replaced by a 'competent' headquarters' staff, which would assist the chief. His argument was that 'the anomaly of having a president instead of a military chief at the head of their organisation was ludicrous' in a movement that was now 'essentially a military one'.[200] The motion and its adoption may well have been choreographed beforehand by the John Mitchel Circle. Hobson and Markievicz had grown apart since 1909 and shared a mutual wariness that would not have been uncommon between IRB and Citizen Army members. Martin revealed how the IRB ensured that they could operate 'caucus control' over Markievicz, and circumnavigate any ideas they did not favour:

> the practice was to hold a meeting of [the John Mitchel] Circle with the country delegates attending on the eve of the Ard Fheis and at this meeting all matters of policy were decided, the agenda of the Ard Fheis was examined and discussed and decisions were arrived at before the Ard Fheis met. Certain resolutions of no great importance were left open for free voting but apart from the discussion arising out of these the rest was all so much eye-wash.[201]

A similar strategy may have been implemented in 1915.

Hobson spoke against the abolition of the presidency. His public position was that 'there was a civil side in the Fianna which was of even greater importance than the military one'.[202] Colbert was in agreement with Hobson on this issue, and contended that the character building and citizenship training, the self-governing nature of the enterprise, was even more important than drill or musketry, and that the proposals would place the emphasis solely on the martial.[203]

Colbert's position on the matter suggests that he regarded

the moral purpose of the movement as being just as important as the military. Hobson's stance may have been a pretence, however, a pre-arranged adoption of the role of devil's advocate. Alternatively, in the knowledge that the IRB was determined to strike before the end of the war, he may have feared that Clarke and MacDiarmada would draw Na Fianna into a premature insurrection.

Deliberations resulted in a compromise. Markievicz's position as president was retained and the *ard-choisde* was instructed to appoint an *ard fhéinne* (Fianna chief) and headquarters' staff at its first meeting. The twelve elected to the *ard-choisde* included Hobson, Ó Riain, Martin, Colbert, Heuston and Barney Mellows. Hobson's man Ó Riain was subsequently appointed chief scout.[204] The militarisation of Na Fianna only intensified thereafter.

The Royal Commission on the Rising found that Tom Clarke and fellow Fenian veteran John Daly were at the centre of the 'inner circle by which the plans for insurrection were no doubt matured'.[205] The triumvirate of Daly, Clarke and Seán MacDiarmada were one of the main catalysts of the Rising, and the Daly household was a hub of significant seditious activity. In December 1915, the police learned from an informant that 'prominent extremists and Irish Volunteers recently met at Limerick to discuss the proposal to strike a blow for Irish Independence' and that they were awaiting the opportunity they believed the conscription scare would afford them in the form of popular support.

It is well known that Clarke and MacDiarmada spent Christmas 1915 with the Daly family, and that Easter Sunday was decided on as the date of the Rising around this time.[206] What is less well known is that Colbert was in their company for some of this period. Madge Daly described 'an incident which took place on Christmas Eve, 1915, [which] adequately portrays Con's consideration for others'. Colbert had travelled from Dublin by the night mail and arrived in Limerick about 3am:

> As he was not expected in Limerick, we did not wait up for him, but rather than disturb us, Con walked the streets during that cold winter's night and knocked only when he saw a light in one of the windows. The maids were then going to early Mass so he entered the kitchen, made tea, loaded a tray, and surprised us all with an early cup. Laughing and joking, he did not look the least like a man who had worked all through Christmas Eve, travelled until three o'clock in the morning and then walked the streets for another five hours.[207]

There is no suggestion, however, that Colbert was privy to the intimate detail of Clarke and MacDiarmada's plotting. As recently as mid-1915, his only instructions were that 'he was to guard the line of the Shannon in the event of a rising', as he enthusiastically recounted to a fellow

Volunteer during manoeuvres in Tipperary.[208] He had no more meaningful knowledge until much closer to Easter 1916.

Colbert spent his August 1915 holiday in Athea.[209] Christmas 1915 marked Colbert's last visit home, and he made it a productive one, swearing his brother Jim into the IRB and also the local schoolteacher and Volunteer commander, William Danaher. Colbert took the opportunity to put the local company through a series of drill exercises. He left a bilingual Christmas card for his sister Katty.[210] As many as 3,000 people attended commemorative ceremonies for Colbert in Athea in 1966. Kevin Danaher, son of William, recounted stories of Colbert's sojourns in the village:

> he could not walk along the road without an armed constable following him and noting his movements and his contacts. Another man might have been angered by this, but Con Colbert possessed a keen sense of humour, and many stories are told of jokes which he played on these unwanted attendants, such as the story of the day when he discovered a 'peeler' lurking in a clump of furze bushes, and Con, with the most innocent air in the world, set up a target on the bush and had a little rifle practise which put the unfortunate constable in fear of his life. Another story of this kind concerns my own parents ... One very cold and wet evening he came to our house to show my

mother his fine new Volunteer Captain's uniform, and while they were drinking tea the servant girl came in to tell them that 'there was a poor amadan of a peeler stuck under a bush outside at the gate and the rain down on top of him in buckets', whereupon my mother, very much to Con's amusement, told her to bring the peeler into the kitchen and give him a cup of tea while he was waiting, with the assurance that he would be told when it was time to take up his duty again.[211]

Chapter 5

The Rising

The only change to Colbert's regular routines in the opening months of 1916 was an increase in the intensity of his activity. He was still attending to matters such as recruiting Fianna members and swearing them into the IRB.[212] All seven members of the Military Council of the IRB (the same seven signatories of the Proclamation – Tom Clarke, Éamonn Ceannt, James Connolly, Seán MacDiarmada, Thomas MacDonagh, Patrick Pearse and Joseph Plunkett) were provided with bodyguards from the point when the insurrection policy was agreed at the end of the previous year. Colbert was appointed to Pearse, but his services were never required. For over a month before Easter there was a renewed recruitment drive and

> … a spurt was put on to encourage the men to get their hands on service rifles and .303 ammunition. These could be bought from British soldiers who were returning on leave from France and other war zones. Prices ranged from

£3 to £7 per rifle and if a soldier was drunk enough we relieved him of his rifle without any compensation. A lot of this was done because every Volunteer had to buy his own firearm and ammunition.[213]

As well as infantrymen, arms were sourced from gunsmiths, private owners, second-hand shops and commercial explosive dumps. The general practice was that Volunteers subscribed a few pence per week towards expenses. Those who could afford to do so bought their own uniform, equipment, boots, arms and ammunition. Otherwise, the company advanced money for these purposes and it was repaid in instalments. Henry Murray of A Company, 4th Battalion, was probably one of the better turned-out Volunteers. As Company Adjutant up to December 1915, his uniform consisted of a green tunic with blue facings and brass buttons with a harp design, green breeches, green puttees and a cap with a black glazed peak. He was armed with a Lee-Enfield rifle and bayonet. He had 100 rounds of .303 ammunition. His equipment included a leather belt, leather bandolier, haversack, water-bottle, trench tool and whistle. He also carried a notebook and field dressing. Following his promotion to Lieutenant, he had to provide at his own expense a tunic of the officer pattern, a Sam-Brown belt and a .380 revolver with 50 rounds of ammunition.[214]

Hobson advocated an insurrection only in specific circumstances. If Germany provided enough assistance to

guarantee military success, or if Britain attempted to suppress the Volunteers, he favoured a guerrilla campaign. There
was a general intuition as to what was coming, but Martin
was one of the first Fianna members, on the Sunday before
Easter, to get any 'definite information' on the plan. Reflecting on Hobson's position, Martin acknowledged that it was
sound and practicable, but suggested that something else was
needed:

> I believe that Pearse's doctrine, no matter how impractica-
> ble from the military aspect, had a greater appeal for those
> who had become tired of waiting for favourable opportu-
> nities. And I think it was generally felt that the European
> War which had been going on for eighteen months might
> end without any attempt being made to take advantage of
> England's difficulty, that this would be shameful and disas-
> trous, and that even a glorious failure would be better than
> no attempt at all.[215]

The IRB's plot for an insurrection culminated in the
Easter Rising of 1916. With England's embroilment in
international war they had their opportunity; in the Irish
Volunteers and Citizen Army they had their instrument of
rebellion. The abettors of the uprising had envisaged national
revolt, but this did not materialise. Patrick Pearse's final manifesto of Easter week asserted that the Military Council of the
IRB had planned a general mobilisation and simultaneous

rising of Irish Volunteer companies throughout the country on Easter Sunday. Yet the Volunteers of just four counties – Dublin, Wexford, Galway and Louth – rose in arms. Only fragmentary documentary evidence exists of detailed plans for a countrywide rising. Most of this relates to the landing and distribution of arms from Germany. Orders were couched in vague, generalised terms about 'holding lines', such as Colbert had received before mid-1915.

The report of the Royal Commission on the Rising commented admiringly on the military planning and implementation of the Dublin insurrection.[216] Here again, however, the evidence is incomplete, much of it having gone to the grave with the executed rebels. It seems plausible that the Rising, as it occurred on Easter Monday, was a modified version of what had been planned for Sunday, that the rebel forces were smaller than envisaged and that this skewed the pattern and nature of the military action.

The Rising was the creation of the Military Council of the IRB. Neither the Supreme Council of that organisation, nor the Volunteer Chief of Staff, Eoin MacNeill, were privy to their scheme. Their strategies were based on the assumption that the IRB would be able to commit the whole Volunteer organisation to a revolt, including MacNeill. MacNeill, however, saw the role of the Volunteers as strictly defensive, unless the government attempted to disarm them or enforce conscription.

Clarke and MacDiarmada believed that the betrayal of plans by spies and informers had contributed heavily to the failure of previous revolutionary efforts. With this in mind, they set out to maintain a conspiracy within a conspiracy. All the members of the Military Council, with the exception of Clarke, who deliberately stayed in the background, were on the central executive of the Volunteers. Pearse, Director of Organisation, Joseph Plunkett, Director of Military Operations, and Éamonn Ceannt (from August 1915), Director of Communications, were on the General Council. However, the IRB men around the country did not know that they were to follow only the instructions of this clique at the critical moment. In the end, the manipulation practised by an elite cabal, relying on the unquestioning obedience of a nationwide revolutionary organisation that they kept in ignorance, undermined their object of staging a nationwide rebellion everywhere, except in Dublin, where they were in a position to directly control events.

In fact, the Military Council encountered greater direct opposition to their plans from within the ranks of the Volunteers than they did from the British authorities. And this was despite the fact that they had been more successful in keeping the secret from their own people than from their enemy. The British navy and army had prior knowledge and Dublin Castle, the nerve-centre of the British administration in Ireland, had precise information as to the timing of the Rising, but they vacillated and failed to take pre-emptive action.

The decision to stage the Rising on Easter Monday, forced on the rebel leaders by MacNeill's countermanding order of Saturday which cancelled the 'manoeuvres' planned for Sunday, meant that it was impractical to expect the country at large to rise to any significant extent. Not only were communications inadequate, but the chain-of-command had been severely compromised. The orders distributed to selected officers on Monday could not counteract the effect of repeated eleventh-hour *volte-faces*. The provincial Volunteers were unsure about which orders to follow and what was happening in Dublin, and they did not have the arms they were told they would receive.

It is unlikely that MacNeill's countermanding order alone stopped many Volunteers who wanted to fight from participating in the Rising, particularly in Dublin. In fact, more turned out on Sunday than on Monday. MacNeill did not sink the *Aud* with its 20,000 German rifles, or corrupt the chain-of-command, but his countermanding order did grievously undermine the already tenuous plans for a nationwide rebellion.[217]

Hoping for the synchronised participation of more than 10,000 Volunteers around the country, who would not be told why they were mobilising, there was a simultaneous need to ensure that these men would not be shocked into inaction and to compensate for the suggestions by Hobson and MacNeill that the Volunteers may not have to fight. Áine Ceannt asked her husband Éamonn 'if the men knew the position':

> ... he told me that the Volunteers, certainly his Battalion, had been warned repeatedly that some day they would go out not to return. 'In the present case', he said, 'we could not risk telling the men that the fight will be on tomorrow, as at the time of the Fenian Rising as soon as the men were told about it they thronged the churches for Confession, and the authorities, knowing a lot of the men, suspected that something was going to happen and immediately took action'.[218]

Colbert left little room for confusion about what he understood would be involved when he discussed a possible insurrection with F Company, 4th Battalion:

> Lecturing one night in Emmet Hall he warned those present who numbered about 30, that if there was anyone in their Company who was afraid to die they should make up their minds by the coming week as to their future intentions.

Colbert 'did not intend wasting his own time and theirs unless they made up their minds definitely as to their action when "the day came"'.[219] While Colbert seems to have been fully prepared to lose his life, his single-mindedness did not make him oblivious to the practical concerns of some of his men, who may have had families to support, and were worried about losing their jobs, not to mention dying. Shortly before the Rising, he sought Pearse's advice on those Volunteers who feared for their employment prospects if they took part in a rebellion. Pearse, apparently contemptuously, replied that anyone who was suffering from such misgivings should simply not participate.[220]

The social dimension of cultural nationalism facilitated more open interaction between young men and women than would otherwise have been the case. Many Cumann na mBan members and Volunteers all over the country became partners, and often married. A weekly ceilí might have presented the best opportunity to mingle without the stifling presence of parents or priests.

Colbert was a regular visitor to the Cooney house in Inchicore, where his lieutenant, Christy Byrne, lived. Just weeks before the Rising, he presented Annie Cooney with his portrait:

> He took two photographs out of his pocket and asked me: 'Would you care to have one of these?' One of the photos was of himself alone and the other of himself and Liam Clarke. I said I would be delighted and he actually gave me both … I was charmed because, to tell the truth, I thought an awful lot of him and, of course, he must have known it. He was not, however, at all interested in girls; he was

entirely engrossed in his work for Ireland and devoted all his time to it. He had taken me to a few ceilís and concerts and always brought me home. There would be others in the party. He said, rather significantly: 'Would you mind very much if anything happened to me in this fight that is coming on?' I said I would indeed, 'why do you ask?' He answered: 'I might just be the one to be killed'.[221]

Colbert had shared a similar conversation with Seán Brady:

Con was in a serious mood. 'I know the fight must come soon', he said, 'and I will be in it. I could fall in love with a girl as quickly as anyone, but I know what my fate will be, and I have no intention of bringing that sorrow on any girl'.[222]

Brady's recollections occasionally lean in the direction of hyperbole but if this reported exchange can be taken at face value, and Annie Cooney's testimony suggests that it can, Colbert's stance was not just informed by a sense of foreboding, but a realistic and sensitive assessment of his personal situation.

Also shortly before the Rising, his sister Lila accompanied Con to a ceilí. He introduced her to Lucy Smyth, for whom he evidently had great fondness:

In the course of the evening he said to me 'I'll show you the nicest girl in Dublin' ... I think he was in love with her and would probably have married her if he had lived. She was a nice, gentle, refined girl, a member of Cumann na mBan and a great worker in the movement. She afterwards married Tom Byrne of Boer War fame who was also keen on her at the same time. He was Con's rival. After Con's execution I got to know Lucy well and she visited us in my brother's place at Ballysteen near Shanagolden. On one occasion when I visited her own house, she showed me the letters that Con had written to her. It was from reading them that I came to the conclusion that he was in love with her. I heard afterwards from Fr. O'Mahony ... that Con handed him a bulky packet addressed to Lucy when he visited Marrowbone Lane during Easter week. It was to be delivered to her. Lucy never got it and afterwards hearing about it from someone who was present when the packet was handed over, she went to see Fr. O'Mahony about it. I was with her. He told us that when he was taking the packet from Con one of the girls present, probably a member of Cumann na mBan – he said her name was McNamara – took it from him and said she would deliver it as she was going 'there'. I imagine she meant the GPO where Lucy was, I think, during Easter week. We went around to various places and people seeking information about the packet, but it was never located. We spent days and days at this and we were both very disappointed at its loss. Fr. Albert who I think attended Con before his execution came afterwards to me inquiring about Lucy for whom he had a last message from Con. She never told me what it was, nor did I ask her. He was very serious where work for Ireland was concerned and that is why I never thought he was taking an interest in girls. So I was surprised when I found out that he had been writing love letters to Lucy Sm[y]th and thinking very seriously about her. He also gave Lucy a copy-book containing several scraps of paper with poems scribbled on them. I don't know whether they are his own composition. They are all about Ireland and its struggle for freedom and the sufferings it endured from the English.[223]

There is little reason to think that the poems are not Colbert's own work. But whatever about originality, one poem he sent Smyth at Christmas 1915 is anything but romantic:[224]

May sharp swords fall on Ireland's foe,
May all her hills be rifle-lined,
May I be there to deal a blow
For Ireland, Faith and womankind.
God's good mercy, if I fall
And Ireland lives, strongly free.
If I live and Ireland lives,
Oh! God is very good to me.
And may the song of battle soon
Be heard from every hill and vale.
May I be there with the marching men,
Who fight to free our Grainne Mhaol.

The kindest thing that might be said about the poetry is that there are at least some rhyming features and that the imagery is robust. The most interesting element, however, is his reflection on his own likely fate in the second verse. He is prepared to die for the cause of Ireland, but harbours the hope that he will be spared.

On Palm Sunday night, 1916, the central branch of Cumann na mBan held their weekly ceilí in their premises at 25 Parnell Square. Seán MacDiarmada used it to give cover to a meeting of men from the provinces who had been summoned to receive their final instructions for the Rising. Colbert, unaware of MacDiarmada's purpose, criticised its timing during Lent and expressed his dissatisfaction to Kathleen Clarke:

> He was deeply religious and did not think it right. I could not explain the reason for it to him, so I told him not to be so squeamish and to dance while he could, as he might be dancing at the end of a rope one of these days. I feared I shocked him, and I was sorry the minute the words came out of my mouth. I was sorry for having been so flippant, but I was under a great strain at the time.[225]

Despite his objections, Colbert apparently attended the ceilí, and even acted as master of ceremonies. It might also be considered surprising that the band, according to Áine Heron, started to play 'Tipperary':

… a couple who were strangers got up to dance to it. The whole audience started to hiss, and the couple, thinking they were being hissed at, sat down in embarrassment. But Con Colbert apologised to them, explaining that this air, which was associated with the war and the British army of occupation, was not allowed to be played at Irish functions.[226]

Kathleen Daly's sister Madge also met Colbert in the week before the Rising. She suggested that he was 'entering the fight convinced that he was going to his death', but that he retained his usual composure, 'talking of the risks as part of the day's work in the cause for which he lived':

He said that he believed that they would all go down in the fight but that the sacrifice would be well worth while. I disagreed pointing out that Tom Clarke was so full of hope and that he believed that if they had some initial success the youth of the country would flock to their standard. With the whole country up in arms intensive guerilla warfare would probably develop, and England, so hard-pressed to find soldiers to maintain her armies at full stength for the war against the Central Powers, would be unable to provide the additional forces necessary to quell a general Rising in Ireland. Con could not see it that way but he had no doubt about the righteousness of their effort to win freedom, nor about the effects of their sacrifices. He was in

the highest spirits when he left me, glad of the opportunity
to play his part in the struggle.[227]

It is not clear when exactly the details of the Military
Council's plans for rebellion were first revealed to Colbert.
It may have been at a meeting of the Dublin Centres Board
of the IRB at 41 Parnell Square, early in Holy Week.[228] Otherwise, it could have been at a meeting in Kildare Street on
the Monday or Tuesday, at which Ceannt, Clarke, Connolly,
Pearse, MacDonagh, Major John McBride and Ned Daly
were also present. Colbert informed Bob Holland that 'the
time is near ripe' on the same night.[229] Eamon Martin's recollection was that he received a specific assignment for the
Rising from Colbert at an IRB meeting in Dawson Street
(where Volunteer Headquarters was located) on the Monday
night.[230]

In the previous few weeks Colbert had been detailed
by Ceannt to build up stocks of ammunition. No matter
how minor the quantity, it was eagerly sought. One expedition brought him to Monasterevan, where he secured some
Howth stocks from the local Redmondite Volunteers.[231]
Colbert spent much of the week before the Rising clearing
depots and arranging for the distribution of arms, ammunition and explosives. There were a number of automatic
pistols in circulation, and Colbert secured one of these as his
personal weapon for the Rising.[232]

He had emphasised to Holland that 'You have a job to do

and from now on there must be no slip-up'. His instructions to Holland were to 'Go to Wellington Barracks, South Circular Road, and time yourself from there to the Cork Street gate of Ardee Street Brewery'. This was part of the preparation for the seizure of Watkins' brewery, the position which had been assigned to Colbert's F Company. Holland also had to 'strip the boxes of rifles … and have them fitted up'.

They met again at Dawson Street on Spy Wednesday evening, and Colbert ordered Holland to bring the rifles to the brick works at the Second Lock, Grand Canal, Inchicore, at 8pm on Holy Thursday. F Company was assembled at the Brickfields when Holland arrived: 'There were also some new recruits. There were more men there than usual.'[233] There was a general distribution of arms to F Company. Colbert, wanting to leave as little to chance as possible, instructed Tom Young to reconnoitre their area of operations:

> … comprising the South Circular Road from Wellington Barracks, as it was then called, to Rialto Bridge on the one side, bounded on the other side by … Cork Street, Marrowbone Lane and Ardee Street, and to prepare a sketch map of the locality. I remember he told me to take a day off from work to do it. It did not convey anything to me except I thought it was just another efficiency test, as we were subject to tactical tests at the time.[234]

It is not surprising that Colbert had little time for personal correspondence at this point, but he did manage to send one short letter to Gretta, asking her to convey his wishes for 'a very happy and joyful Easter' to the rest of the family – 'I have not time to write to all' – and to pray for him.[235]

On Good Friday morning Colbert called to Holland's home. He warned Holland to be ready to mobilise, not to leave home under any circumstances apart from direct orders from Colbert himself, and that 'the next mobilisation would probably be the last'. Holland took this to mean that the Volunteers were about to rise. Anxious to ensure the fullest possible turnout, Colbert implored Holland to mobilise

> ... any man that I thought would fight irrespective of whether they were members or past members of the Volunteers. A lot of men had left the ranks of the Volunteers because they thought nothing would ever come of it and these were the men Colbert was referring to.

He conveyed the impression that 'it would be street fighting' and Holland was

> ... to tell the men to bring the principal tools of their particular trades such as hammers, saws, picks, crowbars and such like. Also any man who had a scissors or hair-cutting machine to bring one.

Colbert was concerned that any man who intended on fighting should go to confession beforehand. Before departing, however, he declared with characterisitic passion that even if nobody turned out, he would fight on his own.[236]

Like many prominent Volunteers, wary of the possibility of arrest, Colbert did not spend the nights before the Rising at his ordinary lodgings. From Good Friday, he stayed with the Cooneys and Christy Byrne in Inchicore.[237] This was much more convenient to F Company and the 4th Battalion than his digs in Ranelagh. Byrne also reckoned that Colbert's idea was to enhance their chances of resisting capture: '… if the police did come two of us together would put up a better fight than either of us could do single-handed'.

In preparation for what he thought would be the start of the rebellion, Colbert attended Mass and received absolution on Easter Sunday morning.[238] Following the publication of Eoin MacNeill's countermanding order cancelling the planned 'manoeuvres' in the *Sunday Independent*, and the subsequent Military Council decision to postpone the revolt, the intending insurrectionists found themselves in what must have been a strange vacuum. On the understanding that the mobilisation was suspended, but only temporarily, they had little to do but stand by and await further instructions.

Byrne 'knocked around all day … but nothing happened'.[239] Colbert wanted to have the officers and men 'together in case of urgent necessity', and most of them attended the regular Sunday night ceilí at the local Gaelic League branch in the Cleaver Hall, Donore Avenue.[240]

When it came to the Easter mobilisation, the most zealous Volunteers were excited that the long-awaited rebellion was about to happen and that they would get their chance to engage the enemy. Colbert, who had been working towards this moment for most of his adult life, was eager for action. Seán Brady met him on Easter Monday, the morning of the Rising: '... he was vividly happy'.[241] He attended Mass and took Communion, and '... he told me [Annie Cooney] to have his breakfast ready when he came back. I did so'. Cooney described his delight as he was about to set off from her house with Christy Byrne. Annie and her sister Lily were 'feverishly busy', filling haversacks with whatever food happened to be at hand. Colbert and Byrne were in uniform:

> We helped them to buckle on the haversacks and Sam Brown belts and they were all excited to get out. During the time I was buckling him up Con – who has not a note in his head – was singing 'For Tone is coming back again' he was so excited and charmed that at last the fight was coming off. He thought of nothing else. The pair went off, wheeling their bicycles which were loaded up with pikes, their rifles and small arms.[242]

Colbert was 'full of fight' according to his companion, Byrne.[243]

Colbert's anticipation of the occasion that would allow him to bear arms in pursuit of independence had been such that he recorded it in written form:

Hail! Ye the dawning, hail!
The dawn of blood and steel.
The rise of the Gall and the Gael
For Ireland's Weal.
Be your arms strong and well cared
For the battle for Life is at hand;
So sons of the Gael be prepared;
Reck not ye! strength of the foe.
Remember Emmet the Good
And the fights that were fought long ago.
Think not of sisters or wife
Of sweethearts, of parents, of child.
Think not of mere treasures of life.
Think thoughts of the foe fierce and wild.[244]

He welcomed 'the dawn of blood and steel', the opportunity to fight, and he did not falter in his personal promise. He proved to be more flexible, however, in what he expected of others. 'Think not of sisters or wife, of sweethearts, of parents, of child. Think not of mere treasures of life', he urged. But when it came time to surrender, he did not demand of his followers that they submit to arrest and the risk of imprisonment or worse.

On Easter Monday morning, 24 April 1916, the Dublin

brigades of the Irish Volunteers, troops of Na Fianna, dozens of the women of Cumann na mBan, the Irish Citizen Army and a handful of members of the Hibernian Rifles mustered at various points around the city.[245] The rebels, around 1,600 in total, occupied a ring of prominent buildings, fortified them, and awaited the arrival of British soldiers.

James Connolly, Patrick Pearse and Joseph Plunkett marched from Liberty Hall to the GPO. The elderly Clarke and the disabled MacDiarmada travelled by car. Ned Daly's 1st Battalion mobilised at the Gaelic League Hall on Blackhall Street and proceeded to the Four Courts. The 2nd Battalion under Thomas MacDonagh and Michael O'Hanrahan assembled at St Stephen's Green before garrisoning the nearby Jacob's Factory. The majority of the 3rd Battalion, under Éamon de Valera, rendezvoused at an old school, St Andrew's on Great Brunswick Street, from where they occupied Boland's Mills and Westland Row railway station in the south docks. Éamonn Ceannt marshalled the 4th Battalion at Emerald Square, off Cork Street, just north of Dolphin's Barn, and announced that their enterprise had received the Pope's blessing.[246] Their main deployment was to the South Dublin Union. Seán Heuston led a small detachment of men and boys to the Mendicity Institution. Commandant Michael Mallin and Lieutenant Constance Markievicz of the Citizen Army seized the College of Surgeons and St Stephen's Green.

Battle raged throughout the centre of Dublin, but the army's superior numbers and firepower overwhelmed the resistance by the weekend. The lack of documentary corroboration of the Military Council's exact intentions means that questions abound about their military strategy. It remains difficult to understand why positions of little or no tactical significance, such as St Stephen's Green, were prioritised, while sites of definite tactical and emblematic value, primarily Trinity College, were ignored (nonetheless, one of the most powerful impacts of the Rising was in revealing fissures in imperial structures and illustrating how the established order was propped up by psychological as well as physical scaffolds).

The South Dublin Union, the largest poorhouse in the country, with over 3,000 ill and destitute inmates, and its own churches, stores, canteens and hospitals, was garrisoned when there were equally viable alternatives. Surely this vulnerable community did not have to be turned into a combat zone? Éamonn Ceannt explained that the Guinness brewery would not be occupied by the 4th Battalion because its vastness meant it would be impossible to garrison and because there was no food in it.[247] But these issues applied to many of the buildings that the 4th Battalion did eventually sequester.

The issue at stake is the fundamental purpose of the Rising. Were the rebels resolved to stage a *coup d'état* and to establish a republican state, or were they resigned to failure but determined to make a gesture of martyrdom, designed to inspire the next generation of freedom fighters and to resurrect the physical-force tradition? The timing of the Rising at Easter carried symbolic connotations, but the fact that it was a holiday weekend also had practical benefits.

Two contrasting principal interpretations of the motivation of the rebels have dominated the historiography of the Rising at various points. A powerful but simplistic nationalist narrative quickly established itself, depicting a valiant struggle by sefless patriot heroes in a noble cause, and a spiteful reaction from a malevolent and oppressive British empire. This version held sway, virtually unchallenged, for several decades. When a more nuanced corpus of research seemed set to emerge in the late 1960s and early 1970s, the eruption of concerted violence in Northern Ireland confounded matters. The political crisis presented academics with the dilemma of whether to pursue abstract understanding or to mobilise scholarship against militants. Rather than correcting national foundation myths, which had played a vital role in the process of state-building, some of the new history simply replaced old nationalist teleologies with different distortions.

The conspiratorial nature of the Military Council, and the democratic credentials or otherwise of the rebellion, desperately needed to be analysed, as did its military shortcomings. However, insinuations that the leaders deliberately maximised civilian losses so as to ratchet up Anglophobia were terribly imbalanced. In this inversion of the original plot of heroic self-sacrifice, it was ordinary Dubliners, the residents of the inner-city slums and tenements, who were sacrificed for the nation at the behest of a fanatical, blood-thirsty elite.

There were approximately 450 fatalities during the week, and nearly three times that many were wounded. Over half of those killed were civilians, whereas Crown forces consti-tuted less than one-third and rebels (including those subse-quently executed) less than one-fifth. In areas where British troops suffered heavy casualties or encountered stiff resist-ance, the soldiers appear to have regarded everyone as a legit-imate target. The fact that many Volunteers were without a uniform complicated matters further, but the arena of the densely populated inner city meant that civilian casualties were inevitable in any case.

The Military Council's decision to stage their insurrection in this urban setting may have contradicted their image of themselves as a conventional military force following stand-ard procedures, but when the colonial realities of the situ-ation are taken into account, it carried irrefutable military logic. The dismayed response of Pearse and his fellow leaders to the suffering of civilians at the end of the week strongly suggests a lack of foresight, as opposed to a cynical scheme to inflict carnage on the population.[248]

Bob Holland had finally received confirmation that mobilisation was proceeding from Tom Young at about 7am on Easter Monday. Their aim was to maximise the number of Inchicore men at Emerald Square, the designated rally point for the 4th Battalion.[249] Peadar Doyle, whom Colbert had earlier appointed as staff orderly to Commandant Éamonn Ceannt and Vice-Commandant Cathal Brugha, arrived at 10am. He found only a policeman waiting for him:

> I will leave it to your imagination as to how one could or
> should feel under the circumstances, parading for about half
> an hour attired in a semi-military uniform, fully armed and
> 500 rounds of ammunition, etc., and your only companion
> a policeman.[250]

Between 100 and 150 Volunteers, and probably just over thirty members of Cumann na mBan, had gathered in the square by 11.30am.[251] D Company Lieutenant James Kenny's recollection was of 'a poor turnout so far as numbers went, taking into account the strength of the Battalion at the time'.[252] On a 'gloriously fine' day, no blame could be apportioned to the weather for the mediocre response of the rank and file, as it was, for instance, in Limerick.[253]

At the outset, Colbert was slightly deflated by the paucity of the response to the restructured mobilisation from Na Fianna and the Volunteers. He remarked to Bob Holland that 'if they had turned out we would need no outside assistance'. Despite his disappointment, however, he still gave the impression that 'if only one had turned out with him he would have carried on'.[254] Only a fraction of the 4th Battalion men who had trained on Holy Thursday reported for duty on Easter Monday.

Éamonn Ceannt was in command and, along with his fellow officers, he wore full uniform. Most of the men were in part-uniform. Holland, for instance, wore mufti with knickerbockers, long stockings and leggings. Weapons included Howth Mausers and old Lee-Enfield rifles, a variety of shotguns and revolvers, swords and bayonets, and even pikes 'of the crudest kind'.[255] These pikes were not necessarily solely symbolic, however. A batch that had been manufactured at Inchicore railway works were used in breaking in the doors of the various buildings occupied by the 4th Battalion.[256]

Colbert appointed a six-man cyclist party, including Bob Holland and Tom Young, to safeguard his advance to Ardee Street. Their task was to survey British military activity in the area which Young had recently mapped, i.e., between Wellington Barracks and Watkins' brewery, which lay east of the South Dublin Union. They were to observe the gate of Wellington Barracks and prevent any deployment of troops in numbers. Nothing unusual had occurred by midday, so they proceeded to rejoin their comrades.[257]

At about 11.30am, the core of the battalion started for the South Dublin Union.[258] Their main supporting post would be Jameson's Distillery in Marrowbone Lane, with a further outpost at Roe's Distillery, Mount Brown, as well as at Watkins' on Ardee Street. Éamonn Ceannt's force followed the sliver of the Grand Canal which flowed to James' Street Harbour, adjacent to the Guinness Brewery. They passed the Rialto Bridge at noon and walked through the southern ingress of the South Dublin Union. 'Persons desiring to leave were permitted to do so. The gates were then bolted.' One of the nuns wondered if they had come to read the gas meter.[259]

The fifty acres of the Union included a miscellany of buildings and extended north almost to where James' Street intersected with Steven's Lane. Its size and location presented an immovable impediment to the movement of British forces. Captain Seamus Murphy, the battalion adjutant, remembered Ceannt earlier 'describing with enthusiasm how from the South Dublin Union we could control or stop the troops entering the city from Richmond Barracks' in Inchicore, west of the centre.[260] What it could not control or stop, however, was the arrival of reinforcements to Kingsbridge Station, which lay to its southwest, from the Curragh and other southern garrisons. Neither could it do anything to prevent the advance of troops from barracks in west Dublin.

As well as its other concerning and complicating factors,

the scale of the Union compound stretched Ceannt's force beyond their capabilities. With a variety of stragglers complementing his original number, Ceannt had probably somewhere between 150 and 180 men under his command. Given the dimensions of the Union, and the tactics and weapons of the day, he would have needed many times this number to hold the whole perimeter. It is not clear if it would have been possible to evacuate all the inmates, or even whether this would have been more desirable than allowing them to be caught up in the fighting.

Bob Holland, meanwhile, had experienced a series of misadventures in the earlier part of the day, which illustrate the slightly haphazard nature of the Volunteer enterprise that morning. Circumstances prevented him from joining up with Colbert at his command in Ardee Street. Colbert's occupation of Watkins' had not been completely unopposed. Reporting at midday to the brewery as ordered, Holland encountered what he categorised as a 'very rowdy crowd of women of the poorer class'. They were probably the wives and dependents of men who had enlisted in the British army. To vent their antagonism to the 'Sinn Féiners' who had manhandled the caretaker of the brewery, the mob were assaulting the Volunteers at the main gate (Tom Young's account of what may have been the same incident describes how 'the ladies pulled us off the bicycles and we had to use the butts of our rifles to defend ourselves').[261]

Holland's efforts to make himself known to his colleagues in Watkins' failed, and he could not get into the post. He did, however, encounter two Volunteers, one of them his brother Dan, carting a load of guns, ammunition and tinned food to the garrison. Rather than attempting to run the gauntlet of the incensed women, they returned up Cork Street with the supplies and left the cart in a yard at Dolphin's Barn. Holland then returned to Marrowbone Lane and managed to make contact with the 4th Battalion's secondary post, Jameson's Distillery. Jameson's lay just across the canal from the South Dublin Union, but was a much more manageable base. Holland next backtracked to Dolphin's Barn for a second time. Collecting his colleagues and their cart of supplies, they once again proceeded the quarter of a mile down Cork Street, this time 'at top speed, running', because they could hear the sound of gunfire coming from near the canal. Unlike the Grand Old Duke of York, whose tactics Holland seemed to be replicating, his marching up and down was eventually successful. At 3pm, his small party entered Jameson's to cheers from the Volunteers, who were 'all in good spirits'. They were preparing for a siege by filling a large vat with fresh water.[262]

The clash between the 'very rowdy crowd of women' and the 'Sinn Féiners' at Watkins' was not an isolated or unique incident. At the nearby Roe's Distillery, just to the north of the South Dublin Union, across Mount Brown, a twenty-three-strong C Company section faced opposition from civilians even before the military response began. The rear entrance of Roe's was at Bow's Bridge, which led to the Royal Hospital at Kilmainham, headquarters of the British army in Ireland, just a couple of hundred yards away. Local residents were irate at the blockading of the bridge. 'The women spat at us and shouted jingo slogans', recalled Patrick Egan, 'while the men started to pull down the barricade'. Captain Thomas MacCarthy recalled being 'practically attacked by the rabble' while trying to break down the back gate: 'I will never forget it as long as I live. "Leave down your ----ing rifles", they shouted, "and we'll beat the ---- out of you". They were most menacing to our lads.'[263]

Knocking out ordinary Dubliners by clubbing them with their rifles may not have been the ideal start to the rebellion for the Volunteers of C Company, but they were not the only ones who had such an experience. If the ojective behind the occupation of Roe's was to strengthen the northern defences of the South Dublin Union, it failed. Its three storeys did not command the Union grounds to the front, and were overlooked by the Royal Hospital to the rear. Not only that, but its windows were set in such a way that they were compromised as vantage points, and simultaneously left the defenders unprotected. Another huge problem was that C Company had only 300 rounds of ammunition between them. By Tuesday, their 'few sandwiches … had long disappeared. A slug from the water bottle was now all that was left'. No arrangements had been made for cooking. Repeated efforts to contact Ceannt in the Union were frustrated. Although there was no direct British assault on Roe's, and the men 'felt fairly safe within'[264], Thomas McCarthy decided that 'continued occupation of this post would have served no useful military purpose'. He was also confronted by the bare fact that 'we had no food'. C Company evacuated and dispersed, and 'it was a case of every man for himself'. Some of the men went home; some reported to Marrowbone Lane.[265]

Colbert, meanwhile, was ensconced in Ardee Street, but with 'less than a score' of Volunteers.[266] Fifteen or so F Company men had gone originally to Jameson's, a much larger building.[267] Shortly after occupying Watkins', he sprained his ankle jumping off a barrel, and was apparently limping and in some pain for the rest of the week. Seán Brady suggested that before the surrender, Colbert exchanged his heavy military boots for the dancing slippers of a Fianna boy who had been expecting to attend a ceilí, and that Colbert was wearing the slippers when he was executed.[268] Colbert may have been the only Volunteer to sustain any injury in Watkins', because apart from a passing exchange with British troops advancing towards the city centre from Richmond barracks on the Monday, the outpost was quiet.

Early on Wednesday morning, however, probably at some point between 4am and 6am, Colbert reinforced the larger garrison in Jameson's distillery, on Marrowbone Lane. What

The Provisional Government

... TO THE ...

CITIZENS OF DUBLIN

The Provisional Government of the Irish Republic salutes the CITIZENS OF DUBLIN on the momentous occasion of the proclamation of a

Sovereign Independent Irish State

now in course of being established by Irishmen in Arms.

The Republican forces hold the lines taken up at Twelve noon on Easter Monday, and nowhere, despite fierce and almost continuous attacks of the British troops, have the lines been broken through. The country is rising in answer to Dublin's call, and the final achievement of Ireland's freedom is now, with God's help, only a matter of days. The valour, self sacrifice, and discipline of Irish men and women are about to win for our country a glorious place among the nations.

Ireland's honour has already been redeemed; it remains to vindicate her wisdom and her self-control.

All citizens of Dublin who believe in the right of their Country to be free will give their allegiance and their loyal h-lp to the Irish Republic. There is work for everyone: for the men in the fighting line, and for the women in the provision of food and first aid. Every Irishman and Irishwoman worthy of the name will come forward to help their common country in this her supreme hour.

Able bodied Citizens can help by building barricades in the streets to oppose the advance of the British troops. The British troops have been firing on our women and on our Red Cross. On the other hand, Irish Regiments in the British Army have refused to act against their fellow countrymen.

The Provisional Government hopes that its supporters—which means the vast bulk of the people of Dublin—will preserve order and self-restraint. Such looting as has already occurred has been done by hangers-on of the British Army. Ireland must keep her new honour unsmirched.

We have lived to see an Irish Republic proclaimed. May we live to establish it firmly, and may our children and our children's children enjoy the happiness and prosperity which freedom will bring.

Signed on behalf of the Provisional Government,

P. H. PEARSE,

Commanding in Chief the Forces of the Irish Republic, and President of the Provisional Government.

Manifesto read by Patrick Pearse from the GPO on Tuesday, 25 April 1916.

Above: British soldiers at a barricade of barrels.

Below: A carbon-duplicated script of the order written by Colbert at 11.28am on Easter Monday, 1916, relaying the direction of Éamonn Ceannt to Lieutenant Boland to 'Act as advanced Guard to 4th Batt. only.'

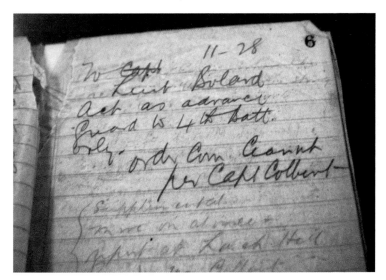

The aftermath: A view of the destruction of the city centre from the top of Nelson's Pillar, looking east over North Earl Street.

Left: A British officer holding the captured 'Irish Republic' flag.

Centre: A British soldier disposing of pikes used by the rebels during the Rising. Pikes symbolised continuity with earlier rebellions. Their practical effect was limited, but the 4th Battalion did employ them in gaining entry to buildings.

Bottom: British soldiers enjoying a drink in Trinity College, in the middle of Dublin.

Above: 1st Battalion, Fifth Fusiliers, Rawalpindi, 1910. Lieutenant Colonel Douglas Sapte, who presided over Colbert's court martial, is seated third from left, with monocle.

Below: Prime Minister Asquith arrived in Dublin on 12 May, the day of the final executions. Here he is leaving Richmond Barracks.

Above: Colbert's letter to his sister Lila, written just hours before his execution.

Below: Irish National Aid Association and Volunteers Dependants' Fund, 1917, including the Cooney sisters Annie and Lily, Rose McNamara and Lucy Smyth.

CORNELIUS COLBERT
(Who took a prominent part in the Rebellion),
Executed May 8th, 1916.

Cornelius Colbert memorial postcard.

Unveiled in 1938 on Sarsfield Bridge, Limerick city, this monument includes portraits of Ned Daly, Tom Clarke and Colbert, as well as the feminised Mother Ireland, her broken shackles being loosened by Colbert. Rifle in hand, Clarke points to the Proclamation.

most likely happened is that Colbert, realising that the brewery on Ardee Street held little tactical significance, resolved to relocate his contingent to where they could contribute more directly.

Whether or not his decision was confirmed by an order from a more senior officer is uncertain, and a variety of sources provide contrasting accounts. Contact could not be established with Ceannt, but the matter may have been discussed with Thomas MacDonagh or John MacBride in Jacob's.[269] By Christy Byrne's reckoning,

> Con sent a written message to James Connolly in the G.P.O. on Tuesday, to the effect that his men were not engaged and had nothing to do except erect barricades since they occupied their position at ten a.m. on Monday. They did not even see any enemy troops. A reply, in typescript, was received from Connolly about mid-day on Tuesday to the effect that the entire garrison of Ardee Street Brewery was to go to Marrowbone Lane to reinforce Seamus Murphy and his men who were being hard pressed by the military.[270]

Bob Holland asked Colbert why he had left Watkins', and 'he said it was not an important post and covered nothing of any strategic importance'.[271] It was simply too remote from the South Dublin Union to contribute to its defence, and was too large for his small garrison to hold securely.

There may have been another factor behind the transfer

from Watkins', however. Seamus Kenny, Quartermaster of the 4th Battalion, suggested that hunger came into the equation:

> During the week, about Wednesday or Thursday, Con Colbert's crowd in Ardee Street distillery had no food, and were dying with hunger, and they sent word to us [in Marrowbone Lane] would we take them in and we said yes. They came at about four o'clock that morning.[272]

One of the garrison was apparently able to go home before the move and collect some civilian clothes and overcoats from his mother. This was to aid Colbert and the others who were in uniform to pass through the streets without attracting too much attention.[273] So that their boots would not be heard, they supposedly went 'in their stockinged feet'.[274] Whether or not these efforts at avoiding detection made any appreciable difference, or even happened at all (one of those present stated that they fixed bayonets), the column marched to Marrowbone Lane without incident.[275] Byrne was at its head, and Colbert at the rear.[276] When Colbert arrived he was 'all smiles although he looked very tired'. His good humour might have deserted him, however, if he had known that one of the Jameson's garrison had just returned from an expedition to Cork Street for rifles, during which he also managed to drink three pints in a public house.[277]

Captain Seamus Murphy of A Company, Kimmage, and 4th Battalion Adjutant, was originally in charge of Jameson's.

Some of the garrison may have thought of Colbert as the de facto commander, or at least may have given that impression in later years as part of the process of glorifying the executed men, but he was officially subordinate to Murphy. Colbert's greater military acumen may have made him a more compelling presence, however. As far as Bob Holland could gather, 'it was Con Colbert and Harry Murray [Lieutenant Henry Murray of Murphy's A Company] who were giving all the orders'.[278] When Thomas Gay, a runner between garrisons, reported to Marrowbone Lane, he sought out Colbert. In one instance, 'Captain Colbert was resting. I gave the information to Seamus Murphy who was acting in his stead'.[279]

Around 1947, Madge Daly's claim that 'the soul of chivalry always, Con saved the life of his superior officer at the post where he served during the Rising and forfeited his own by assuming command when the surrender came' was published in the Limerick edition of Anvil's popular *Fighting Story* series.[280] This theory had been in circulation since 1916, and had grown fresh legs. Gary Holohan's testimony to the Bureau of Military History suggested that

> When the time came to surrender he [Colbert] volunteered to act as officer in charge instead of Seamus Murphy who was in charge and was a married man. For that brave act he paid the penalty with his life. I was certainly convinced that this story was true at the time and I was in touch with many members of the Marrowbone Lane Garrison.[281]

Holohan may well have been convinced originally, but he should probably have known better by the time he made his statement in 1949. The story had gained some currency, however, and Joseph Reynolds, also in 1949, repeated that Colbert was 'second in command', and only 'took over command at the surrender'.[282] In the same year, Áine Ceannt was determined

> … to deny the canard that has gone around about Seamus Murphy where people said because he was not executed that he had permitted Colbert to take his place as the man in charge of the distillery, thereby saving his own life. This is an absolute falsehood.[283]

Christy Byrne was equally unequivocal:

> Regarding rumours that went around concerning Con Colbert's execution instead of Seamus Murphy, I wish to record that Seamus Murphy was in charge in Marrowbone Lane and Con was second in command. The commands remained so until the surrender.[284]

In any case, there were others factors involved in the decision to execute Colbert, largely to do with his activities before the Rising. At no point in his trial was he accused of holding an independent command.[285] In fact, the evidence ranged against Colbert inaccurately associated him with Jacob's, rather than with Marrowbone Lane or Ardee Street.

Laurence O'Brien was one of the C Company Volunteers who made his way from Roe's to Jameson's. On arrival he was questioned closely. There was some doubt as to the veracity of his story about the evacuation of Roe's. Colbert, however, acting on his own principle that 'a man's word must be taken as absolute truth', declared unequivocally that he was prepared to accept the statement, and the small party was admitted.[286]

The full complement of the Marrowbone Lane garrison was probably about 145. The combined unit incorporated seven Fianna – the younger boys acting as messengers and scouts, the older boys fighting alongside their Volunteer comrades.[287] Twenty-five women of Cumann na mBan had entered Jameson's with Murphy on Monday morning, but three of them had left again before Tuesday.[288] Many of these women were members of the Gaelic League branch at which Bob Holland had attended the ceilí only the night before.[289]

One account suggested that Colbert presided over 'an atmosphere of easy camaraderie and relative equality'.[290] Colbert himself may not have been entirely at ease with the situation, however. Like Ceannt, anticipating bloody fighting ahead, he had refused to permit any members of Cumann na mBan to accompany his detachment from Emerald Square. While the *esprit de corps* and unity of purpose that existed is not in question, whether there was egalitarianism between the genders is another issue. While the women of the Citizen Army and a handful of others did not tolerate the kind of benign sexism that prevailed elsewhere, they were exceptional, and the women in Marrowbone Lane performed roles that were strictly delimited. They were expected to congregate in the main hall 'through the hours of darkness'.[291] Annie Cooney's experience in Jameson's was one shared by the majority of Cumann na mBan members during the Rising: 'our business was to look after the men … our main activity was preparing food and generally looking after the welfare of the men'.[292] Seamus Murphy's wife, Sheila, went to visit him on Tuesday: 'I remained in the distillery and cooked for the Volunteers'.[293] Ellen Sarah Bushell and Mollie O'Hanlon acted as couriers.[294]

Despite now being much closer to the 4th Battalion's main locus, where the fighting was at its most severe, namely the South Dublin Union, as well as commanding approaches from the south and east, Jameson's was largely bypassed by the cordon of British troops that gradually encircled the city centre. As at Watkins', however, the garrison was exposed by a lack of strength-in-depth. Colbert was not deterred by this and, perhaps because of it, stationed his men on the 'most open side to the enemy'.[295] The arrival of F Company had 'put new spirit into the atmosphere of our post', and Colbert also adopted more aggressive tactics than had previously been pursued:

> Up to this the Volunteers' activity had been confined to the interior of the building; sniping from the different points had been kept up intermittently. … Immediately Con Colbert

placed an outpost in an open position on the green sward near the bank of the canal. There was a public road between their position and the canal bank and they lay on the ground. From there they were able to pick off any British soldiers that attempted to enter the Union grounds from the back.[296]

Marrowbone Lane was only sporadically the scene of heavy fighting on the Wednesday, Thursday and Friday, although to Bob Holland it seemed as if the Volunteers and soldiers were locked in 'a battle royal'. Priests heard confessions in the first half of the week, and on Thursday the garrison 'more or less relaxed and the chaps were finding their bearings and making themselves acquainted with the different parts of the buildings'.[297] Christy Byrne recalled that 'we were so free from fighting that Seamus Murphy, the O/C, suggested that we should have a sing-song – to keep the fellows' hearts up'.[298] There was 'very little First Aid work to do', according to Annie Cooney.[299]

While no one was seriously wounded, 'none got much sleep or rest, as attack on a big scale was always expected and prepared for'.[300] Thomas Doyle 'never slept one single hour of that whole week. Once the first two days passed I never thought of sleep, just lived without sleep and never thought of it'.[301] British snipers did sustain an intense if inaccurate barrage, taking cover behind tree trunks, the distillery's walls, and rapidly dug trenches along both sides of the Grand Canal and in adjacent fields:

… no mass formation of soldiers was in sight … [but] some bullets began to come through the windows hitting the inner wall. Splinters of bricks and mortar started to fly and twisted bits of the lead bullets flew around in all directions.[302]

The rebels responded with rifle fire and, after receiving instruction from Colbert, resorted in one instance to hand grenades of dubious reliability. Henry Murray observed grenades being primed by members of the 4th Battalion during Easter week. The process involved

… packing a small meat or tomato can with motor cycle ball-bearings using gelignite as the explosive and inserting a fuse which could be ignited by a match. I saw about 50 of these grenades prepared and they were by no means the formidable weapon that may appear from the description I have given. In fact they were crude, dangerous to handle and of questionable value.[303]

They were apparently effective when called upon in Jameson's, however. The defenders, perhaps even Colbert himself, lobbed at least one grenade over the boundary:

We heard some screeching and shouting outside and a lot of moaning. As a result, the soldiers at the outside of the wall ran away from it and they were fired on by a volley from the distillery. I saw Con Colbert smile as he sent us back into the building again saying 'that stops that attack for the present'. … As night approached again the firing eased off but we could see the bright red glow over the city.

Colbert also issued instructions on the use of 'very crude pikes', constructed from scrap iron salvaged around the brewery. Consisting of a piece of steel with a sharp point, placed atop a broom handle, they were not ultimately used.[304] The British made no concentrated assault on Marrowbone Lane at any point, nor did they turn their artillery on Jameson's.

Volunteers had widely varying levels of aptitude and experience in the handling and use of weapons. Ex-soldiers who became Volunteers benefited from their professional military training, and some had previous experience of warfare, but these were an exception. For the majority of rebels, Easter week provided their first experience of combat.

The Jameson's garrison was not only short on experience, however. They lacked the basic numbers to man the vast rooms of the distillery. Hats were placed on top of brush handles and long sticks in the windows, to draw enemy fire. The most capable riflemen in Jameson's (and there were perhaps as few as fourteen who could have been described as proficient) were given more than one rifle each, either Lee-Enfield Martinis or Howth Mausers. Bob Holland taught two of the women, Josie O'Keeffe and Josie McGowan, how to load these guns and, with their assistance, for the next four days of fighting he exploited an excellent position in one of the grainstores with a commanding westerly view:

> I had grand observation of both north and south sides of
> the canal banks, along the back of the South Dublin Union
> as far as Dolphins Barn bridge … I could see over all the
> roofs of the houses in that area and in the distance a portion
> of the James's Street section of the South Dublin Union.

Josie O'Keeffe had remarked how heavy the Mauser was.
According to Holland, each cartridge was about 6 inches
long and weighed about a quarter of a pound. It had a lead
top, about an ounce-and-a-half in weight, and made very
large entrance and exit holes. He only occasionally used one
of the Howth guns, and was 'driven about 12 feet across the
floor every time I fired it'. He was 'completely blackened'
from the gunpowder:

> When the girls had gone I took off my shirt and left it off
> and put back my coat and waistcoat. Flame about three feet
> long came out through the top of the barrel when it was
> fired and a shower of soot and smoke came back in one's
> face. After three shots were fired from it, it would have to be
> thrown away to let it get cool and the concussion of it was
> so severe that it drove me back along the floor several feet.

One of the women later washed his shirt. The Volunteers
also had to contend with the unfavourable conditions of the
distillery itself: Holland 'felt in a bad way for fresh air … My

nose and throat were bothering me as the dust of the wheat affected them'.[305]

The Na Fianna members, well trained marksmen, inflicted a number of casualties, and decided that it was possible to capture the weapons of the fallen soldiers. Fifteen-year-old Walter Holland (the third of the Holland brothers in Jameson's[306]) told Bob that troops were lying dead in Fairbrothers' field, and that there was an opportunity for them to recover their rifles and ammunition, which were scattered around.

At ten o'clock that night [Wednesday] I [Bob] crossed the wall and landed in a cottage garden next to the Distillery yard where I picked up Walter and Mick Butler [another Fianna member in Jameson's] as arranged, at the entrance to the Back of the Pipes canal end. We crawled into Fairbrothers' field and made very slow progress and the time seemed very long before we picked up the first dead soldier. I cut off his web equipment and one of the others took his rifle. In this manner we stripped quite a lot of dead soldiers. In all we got five rifles. I carried two, Mick Butler carried two and Walter carried one. We tied the web equipment on us and found it very hard to crawl along the ground and not make any noise. We got back to the wall and tapped it to Mick O'Neil on the opposite side. He took over the rifles and ammunition and we went back for another trip. We brought in another five rifles and more ammunition.[307]

As the days passed, the rebels were being gradually worn down. Many were pushed close to breaking point by the almost intolerable pressure exerted on them. Exhausted from lack of sleep, unsettled by the unyielding threat of attack, disconcerted by not only the lack of reliable information and growing isolation but also by the terrifying roar of artillery (even if they were not under direct fire) and the inferno raging through the centre of the city, some did break. Colbert, like the majority of his fellow officers, was previously untested in such extreme conditions. But his self-possession and physical bravery were undimmed, and he demonstrated outstanding leadership. And remarkably, morale generally remained high, albeit unrealistically so and on the basis of misinformation.

If Colbert's men had been 'dying with hunger' in Watkins' brewery, rations were also temporarily an issue in Jameson's. 'There was very little food there ... food was a big problem for a while', recalled Thomas Doyle of F Company. A number of men were tempted by the roasted malt that was abundant in the distillery, and had to be prevented from eating it.[308] There were more luxurious alternatives available at one point, however. It was Bob Holland's nineteenth birthday on 25 April. His brother Walter couriered not just one but two birthday cakes to Jameson's: 'My brother Walter returned with a home-made cake for me [Bob Holland] from my mother for my birthday. He also brought one for Mick Riordan from his mother'.[309]

It was only after a herd of cattle had been driven along Marrowbone Lane that the Volunteers noticed the missed opportunity and realised they needed to be more enterprising in sourcing provisions. Seamus Murphy was aggravated by the missed chance, and asked Tom Young of F Company where he expected to get meat from. Young had been posted as a lookout on the first floor, and did not miss his second chance:

I arranged a system of signals with Sergeant Ned [O']Neill, also of F. Company, who was in charge of the main gate. These signals would indicate to him the type of person wishing to enter, the movements of animals, vehicles and suchlike, the reason being that it was considered unsafe to open the gates without prior knowledge of the person seeking admission, and it was a means of diverting food-stuffs which might be en route to other British garrisons, the Vice-Regal Lodge and suchlike places. … I signalled that there were three cattle being driven along Marrow-bone Lane towards Cork Street. Ned [O']Neill opened the gates and drove the cattle through them. He closed the gates. In a few moments the owner of the cattle came along and stood in consternation. I asked him what his trouble was, and he replied by asking me had I seen three heifers. I, of course, assured him that no cattle had passed that way.[310]

Bob Holland, an apprentice butcher, slaughtered the animals:

> I got a jack-knife and a few penknives and sharpened them
> in the yard on a sandstone. When I had them ready I tied
> up one of the cattle to a winch and killed it with a sledge
> hammer; I dressed it.

Interestingly, Colbert was anxious about the hide of the animal and quizzed Holland about curing it to make mocassins. Holland 'knew nothing about this and he went and started to cure it himself'. This might lend credence to the story that Colbert, after his fall from the barrel in Watkins', was suffering with his ankle and was seeking alternative footwear. According to Áine Ceannt, Sheila Murphy provided medical attention to Colbert, 'as his feet had been badly chafed'.[311] He also 'abominated' holes in his socks, and Annie Cooney mended a pair for him during the week.[312]

A second incident involved a messenger boy who Young spotted peering through the gate of the distillery. Enthused by the sight of trussed chickens in the boy's bicycle basket, Young frantically alerted his comrades. It turned out that the boy, who lived in nearby Dolphin's Barn, was a Fianna member. He worked for a poultry shop, and was supposed to be delivering the chickens, depending on which version of the story you prefer, either to the Vice-Regal Lodge or the officers' mess at Richmond barracks. O'Neill gratefully accepted the gift, and asked Maguire to pass on his compliments to the Lord Lieutenant. Maguire replied, 'For ---- sake, Mister, take the ----ing bicycle as well'.[313] The cooked chickens had to be removed from the pots with bayonets, as there were no other utensils available.[314]

Young recovered from his slow start to perfect the improvised system of requisitioning. Over the week the garrison managed to commandeer one baker's van, a dairy cart with a few churns of milk, 'a load of cabbage', a total of twenty-eight chickens, and the three cows. 'God forgive us,' said Rose McNamara of Cumann na mBan in relation to the cows.[315] She would have been pleased that they did not have to eat the unfortunate horse killed by a startled sentry. It had earlier carried supplies from Keogh's yard near Emerald Square.[316]

On Tuesday, 25 April, Bob heard that 'we are holding the whole City':

> … all the country is marching on Dublin and it is only a matter of a few days until we will have the job done. All we have to do is to keep it up until they arrive.

There was talk that 'the Germans had landed in Galway'. Morale was high, as 'we felt we were winning all around'. The good news kept coming through Wednesday:

> We got word that the city was on fire but that we had only few casualties whilst the British were suffering heavy losses. We certainly believed this, as this was our own case. We had no one killed and only two wounded and these were back in the fight again. If all the garrisons were like ours, and we had no doubt that they were, we were doing very

well indeed. We had only to bide our time. We must win and none of us thought otherwise. Failure was the last thing that I or the rest of us thought of. After reading and thinking over our history of the short quick battles, we could not lose now. We were more than two days and a half fighting and that was longer than four previous rebellions put together. A trickle of reinforcements kept coming in and we were all in high spirits, all young men determined to win and this was our only object. I and the rest of us had made our Easter duty and God would see us on the winning side. I was thinking all about my school days, the lectures that the Christian Brothers gave us each Friday from 12 o'clock to 1 about the Mass Rock and the Famine, of Blessed Oliver Plunkett and of Emmet and Tone …[317]

The wishful thinking continued unabated into Thursday night:

Our dogged spirit is 100% with us all. We are winning and nothing else matters. We will surely get that help. The Germans could not be far from Dublin now and the country Volunteers are showing the way. They have beaten the British in Athlone, Limerick and Galway days ago and they have only to hammer the troops in the Curragh Camp. We have eliminated all the troops that landed at Kingstown and we are only mopping-up the crowd that came down from Belfast. All this is what we were told by the odd stragglers that came in and we readily believed it all as we know that the soldiers we have killed belonged to a varied lot of regiments. We have seen their cap and collar badges. Some of these we have in our possession. The Notts, the Derbyshires, the west Kent's, the Berks, the Wiltshires, the Royal Irish Rifles, the Dublin Fusiliers, the 4th and 5th Hussars, 17th Lancers, South Irish Horse, Enniskilling Fusiliers and Liverpool Rifles, and several others, so we thought there could not be many more left. We knew that Germany was beating England in France and so a few more days wouldn't matter. We carry on with our spirits getting higher.[318]

On Friday morning, the weather was still 'summerlike', but the British presence in the immediate vicinity had decreased. Only cursory 'pot shots' were exchanged. For breakfast, the women 'fried veal cutlets and gave the men a good feed'. Bob Holland was hopeful of having some meat from the beast he had killed for dinner, but he had to make do with a can of soup and some bread made by Cumann na mBan members. He was told that this was more suitable for a Friday, but Rose McNamara enjoyed 'a meat dinner, potatoes, etc.'.[319] Colbert and Holland had time to reminisce about their early days in Na Fianna before British troops reappeared at Rialto bridge at 4pm. After the Rosary finished at 10pm, some of the women raised the idea of 'some kind of music' for Sunday night. There was a determination to maintain certain rituals, and the feeling among the garrison was that 'we were going to be there for a long spell … we hoped that the Germans and the country Volunteers would arrive in time' [before the distillery came under artillery fire].[320]

On Saturday morning, the rebels found to their surprise that the British troops had withdrawn out of range. The speculation was that they were awaiting reinforcements before launching a mass attack. Colbert inspected the Volunteers and otherwise the day was 'uneventful', apart from the capture and questioning of a suspected female spy.[321] Rose McNamara led 'the Captain's [Seamus Murphy's] wife and some of the girls' in searching and interrogating the prisoner:

> We were afraid this person might be a man, in woman's clothes, so we had to be careful as she was a very masculine-looking woman. We each of us had our knives in case of a fight, but she was harmless. We did not find anything on her, so she was let go with a warning.

Afterwards, McNamara, conscious of the need of 'style for Sunday', washed her blouse and 'fell asleep for the first time this week'. Seamus Murphy sent for a priest to say Mass the following day, but this never materialised.[322]

The troops had disappeared from view entirely by Sunday morning, and it started off as 'an easy day', with most of the garrison free to 'ramble all over the distillery'. All the positive rumours were being taken as true:

> We were still in the best of spirits and the girls had baked

some cakes and were getting ready for the ceilidhe in the Main Hall which had previously been cleared. We were looking forward to this …[323]

Murphy (not Colbert, as suggested elsewhere) assembled the garrison at midday, and addressed them 'in the most soul-stirring manner'.[324] There were no complaints about food or sleep. Still anticipating a military assault, he asked

… if they were prepared to fight to the last, even tho' the old enemy whom we were fighting, played her old game and starved us out. They all shouted 'Yes'. He then quoted a passage from history – thus – : 'Greater love no man hath than to lay down his life for his friend' and if all ended well, being Sunday to have a sing song in the evening, to which the brave cailíní were to be invited: cheers from the men.[325]

This scene must have played out before Thomas Gay returned from his sortie to Jacob's. Despite the apparent plenty of Friday, Gay claimed that on Saturday Colbert told him supplies were running out, and that he should go to Thomas MacDonagh in Jacob's to seek bread or anything else that was available. All he found there was news of the surrender. Gay reported back to Marrowbone Lane. Failing to meet Colbert, he informed Murphy of developments. Murphy requested written confirmation, but events made this request redundant.[326]

Communication between Jameson's and other rebel forces

had been minimal for much of the week. Blissfully ignorant of proceedings elsewhere, they maintained a high morale. Henry Murray's contention that the officers of the garrison were extremely dissatisfied with the lack of action and news, and had decided on Friday to move out on Sunday failing the receipt of orders to the contrary, is an intriguing one, but it is not corroborated elsewhere.[327] According to Áine Ceannt's sister Lily O'Brennan, who was in Jameson's, it was Colbert's promise for the Sunday night 'to give the girls a good dinner and a ceilidhe. The garrison had been short of food and the girls left it all for the use of the men'.[328] The Cooney sisters' interpretation was that the ceilí was to be held because it was quiet compared to earlier in the week, and 'we decided to relax': 'Seamus Murphy had given us permission for it if things continued to be all right.'[329] Clearly, Murphy had not ceded complete authority to Colbert. Colbert

> … all the time seemed to think that we must win and said to [Bob Holland] that we must come in at the peace negotiations when the European War had finished. … there was no mention of any of us surrendering at any time.[330]

But beside the fact that attaining belligerent status is usually a frustrated ambition for revolutionary movements, the reality was that the general surrender order had already been issued by Pearse from the GPO the day before, Saturday, 29 April, at about 3.45pm:

In order to prevent the further slaughter of Dublin citizens, and in the hope of saving our followers, now surrounded and hopelessly outnumbered, the members of the Provisional Government present at Headquarters have agreed to an unconditional surrender and the commandants of the various districts in the City and country will order their commands to lay down arms.

It took almost another twenty-four hours before confirmation reached Marrowbone Lane. Developments in the interim, as they had been throughout the week, were highly complex, erratic and often confusing. First-hand accounts are often contradictory in respect of the sequence of events, and do not lend themselves easily to clear exposition.

In the context of Marrowbone Lane, Thomas MacDonagh's contribution to proceedings was the most directly relevant. Father Aloysius and Father Augustine, of the Capuchin Friary in Church Street, accompanied MacDonagh throughout Sunday.[331] Having parleyed with Brigadier-General William Lowe of the British army, and on returning to Jacob's, MacDonagh consulted with his officers and then addressed his men. It was evident to Father Augustine that he was

… suffering a great strain and still held up and spoke bravely for a few minutes telling the men, among other things, that the Volunteers had fought a good fight, held out for one glorious week, and achieved what they meant to accomplish.

Once he announced the surrender, he burst into tears. MacDonagh formally yielded to Lowe at St Patrick's Park shortly after 3pm, handing over his revolver. He also consulted with the South Dublin Union and Marrowbone Lane. At Marrowbone Lane, as recounted by Father Aloysius, a crowd gathered outside while MacDonagh, by now devoid of his Sam Brown belt and sword, and Father Augustine made arrangements with the Volunteers.[332] Aloysius had remained outside with the chauffeur. Discussions were protracted, and Aloysius 'understood they had had some difficulty in persuading the Volunteers there to surrender. They were well fortified and had provisions to last for some time'. Wider circumstances meant that their level of supplies was irrelevant, however, and their vigorous protests were to no avail.

Sheila Murphy judged that 'the men were in splendid spirits throughout. They did not like the idea of surrendering, but when they got the order from their superior officers, they obeyed it without hesitation'.[333] Evidently, the news was a shock, and the mood changed dramatically. Seamus Murphy 'turned a sickly yellow'. Henry Murray 'bowed his head'. Colbert's composure deserted him, though only briefly. He was incredulous and wept openly. He 'could hardly speak as he stood in the yard for a moment or two. He was completely stunned. The tears rolled down his cheeks.' He expressed his bewilderment and disorientation to Holland:

> I do not know what to say or think, but if what I think comes

true our cause is postponed to a future generation. We are
to surrender unconditionally and I cannot forecast what that
will mean. We must have been let down very badly as we have
not had the support of our people that we had expected.[334]

Understandably shaken by the surrender, Colbert's
experience of a hostile public response in the immediate
aftermath would prove crushingly disappointing, and perhaps disillusioning. Bob Holland's recollection of his own
response to the surrender was that 'I felt kind of sick in my
stomach'.[335] Henry Murray suggested that the garrison felt
'deeply humiliated' as a result of not having been as involved
in the fighting as they would have liked.[336] Annie Cooney's
description of the response was also revealing:

> There was dreadful grousing; they were saying 'Was this
> what we were preparing for and living for all this time? Is
> this the end of all our hopes?' They were flinging their rifles
> around in temper and disgust.[337]

Séamus Murphy stated that 'Con [Colbert] was not with
the rest of us when MacDonagh came in'. He described the
general reaction:

> … first of all, surprise – surprise because no major attack
> had been mounted against our outpost, surprise, because
> rumours of great successes for Republican arms had been
> filtering through, rumours that the whole country had

risen, and many other such stories. And, secondly, there was a sense of disappointment among the men – and the women – for we were ready and willing to fight on and had a good supply of arms and ammunition. The matter had to be considered, however, in relation to the most unusual event experienced around Dublin in many, many years and to the mental attitude wrought in men living for one exciting week outside their normal domestic ways. It was not a time that conduced to ordered thought or discussion or favoured opportunities to obtain individual views. With the first indication of the actual position there would, of course, be a lessening of the spirit which had been maintained all during the week. The spirit was still, however, high enough to ensure that if our Commandant [Ceannt], who had our affection and confidence, ordered further resistance, his order would, I am satisfied, have been obeyed.[338]

That most Volunteers declined the ample opportunities that there were to simply stroll away and go home, rather than becoming prisoners, reflected the significance they attached to the principle of military dignity. This was one of the features of the rebellion that would come to be lauded by public opinon. As ever, there were exceptions who chose not to follow the honour system, or did not see a need for it (and adhering to such codes would have been seen as unrealistic folly during the much more successful guerilla campaign of the War of Independence, only a few years later). 'The feeling among many of those in the garrison', according to Thomas Gay, 'was that they would not surrender and some made good their escape because of this feeling'.[339] Colbert asked George Nolan to deliver letters, and advised that he did not need to return to his post.[340] Bob Holland suggested that Colbert presented the option of escape from Marrowbone Lane to anyone willing to take it.[341] This is another indication that Colbert, a single man without a wife or children depending on him, understood that not all of the Volunteers shared the same personal circumstances.

Laurence O'Brien's memory was that 'as the men fell in, one of the junior officers advised that any man without uniform who could should escape quietly', but that Ceannt, by now at Marrowbone Lane, swiftly counteracted that notion. Ceannt stressed that 'we were disciplined troops and would surrender as such. A small number had already taken advantage of the suggestion to get away'.[342] Joe McGrath, future government minister and Irish hospital sweepstakes guru, was one of those who gathered his wits quickly amid the state of general bewilderment. With a cheery 'Toor-a-loo boys, I'm off', he walked out.[343] Annie Cooney recalled that

> There were a few who refused to surrender and they cleared off. It took some time to gather them from all points of the building and to persuade them to obey the order. It was finally brought home to most of them that as soldiers it was their duty to obey the order of their leader.

She was candid in describing Ceannt as 'like a wild man':

His tunic was open, his hair was standing on end and he
looked awful. He evidently hated the task of asking the garrison to surrender. He put his two hands on the barricade,
with his head bent, and presented a miserable appearance.[344]

Many were under the impression that women would neither be searched nor taken prisoner. Murphy and Colbert
'told [the women] to go away home quietly'.[345] Cooney
maintained that the men 'tried to persuade us to go home
but we refused, saying that we would stick it out to the
end … we could have gone away home if we wanted to'.[346]
Ceannt advised his sister-in-law, Lily O'Brennan, to return
home, but she refused.[347] All the women, bar one, obeyed
Rose McNamara's order to surrender with the men.[348]
McNamara described trying to smuggle guns even while in
custody:

We all (22 of us) [one woman having refused to surrender]
gave ourselves up and marched down between two lines of
our brave men. We waited until all the arms were taken away.
The men gave each of us their small arms to do as we liked
with, thinking we were going to go home, but we were not
going to leave the men we were with all the week to their
fate; we decided to go along with them and be with them to
the end whatever our fate might be. Some of the girls had
as many as three revolvers … The sergeant in Richmond

barracks told us we would be searched in Kilmainham, so after a while we reluctantly gave them up to him.[349]

As the women marched behind the men, Margaret Kennedy picked up a rifle and 'carried it the rest of the way but I had to surrender it on orders from the British Officer. The men had to turn everything out of their pockets'.[350]

Ceannt's South Dublin Union garrison came to Jameson's, and the combined forces marched down Marrowbone Lane and through Cork Street, the Coombe and Patrick Street, before turning into Bride Road. Christy Byrne stated that 'when we came out of the Distillery the crowd was cheering us', but this was not generally representative of the reception the defeated rebels received.[351] Bob Holland's memory of being 'subjected to very ugly remarks and cat-calls from the poorer classes' was more typical.[352]

With the exception of the British officer who marched with Ceannt at the head of the column, there was no other escort, and the men were effectively free to disband until they were met by the army at the junction of Patrick Street and Bride Road. There, troops had formed up two deep on each side of the road, with bayonets fixed and machine guns strategically located. The rebels were cordoned off and surrounded. Names were taken, and a note was made of rank and of who was armed before the laying down of weapons, which were then 'swallowed up' by a military lorry. Some of the surrendering Volunteers recalled hearing and seeing sniping at the British forces during the finalisation of formalities.[353] Reference would be made to post-surrender firing at subsequent courts martial.

The Volunteers were escorted to Richmond barracks, the largest in the country, 'the girls singing all the time amidst the insults of the soldiers and the people alone the route'.[354] Upon reaching the barracks, they were jeered at:

> Men, women and children used filthy expressions at us. F Company, which was mainly made up from Inchicore, heard all their names called out at intervals by the bystanders. … 'Shoot the Sinn Féin ….s'. My name [Bob Holland] was called out by some boys and girls I had gone to school with and Peader Doyle was subjected to some very rude remarks. … This was the first time I ever appreciated the British troops as they undoubtedly saved us from being manhandled that evening and I was very glad as I walked in at the gate of Richmond barracks. I had played with some of that mob in my childhood days.[355]

The men and women were separated at Richmond. Just as some senior Volunteers had been determined to exclude women from the Rising, the army was determined not to bring them to trial. Only Constance Markievicz was subequently charged. She was sentenced to death but the court recommended mercy, 'solely and only on account of her sex'.[356]

The prisoners were housed in crowded billets. Naturally enough, they reflected on the week past and contemplated what the future might hold. The possibility that they would be forced into penal units in the British army was aired. Colbert responded, according to Holland's recall (the seemingly perfect clarity of which is difficult to fully credit), that 'from his point of view he would prefer to be executed'. Colbert apparently continued that 'We are all ready to meet our God':

> We had hopes of coming out alive. Now that we are defeated, outside that barrack wall the people whom we have tried to emancipate have demonstrated nothing but hatred and contempt for us. We would be better off dead as life would be a torture. We can thank the Mother of God for her kindness in her intercession for us that we have had time to prepare ourselves to meet our Redeemer.

Colbert then called for a recitation of the rosary 'for the spiritual and temporal welfare of those who fought in the cause of Irish freedom, past, present and future generations'.[357] Despite the failure of the insurgence and the initially unreceptive public reaction, at least some of the leaders appeared confident of vindication. Clarke, MacDiarmada and Plunkett were satisfied that they had started a process that would gain further momentum.[358] Colbert, for his part, seemed initially to have been psychologially overwhelmed by the drama of the surrender. Events were beyond his control, and his expectations had been shattered. Considering his destiny, however, he sought consolation in his religious faith, and it appears that he realised, if not necessarily welcomed, his likely destiny astonishingly quickly, because he cut a much more relaxed and happy figure for the rest of the week. When asked by one of the men what he felt might happen, 'his reply was "for you a long term of imprisonment. For myself, I fear it will be a firing squad"'.[359] He exhibited signs of what might be described as a sense of relief and satisfaction, perhaps even optimism:

> The main body of the prisoners were despondent but the leaders, notably Eamon Ceannt, Major McBride and Con Colbert were resigned and cheerful, their invariable answer to the natural questioning of the men as to their fate being that 'they will probably shoot us and let you fellows off with a few months in jail or internment for the duration of the war'. Eamon Ceannt in particular urged the men in [Henry Murray's] presence to look to the future and not to regard the collapse of the Rising as the end but rather as the commencement of a fresh and better effort; at the same time he expressed his personal view that the surrender was a mistake and that he would have preferred to continue the fight. This attitude of Eamon Ceannt and the gallant, cheerful bearing of Con Colbert impressed the men and an air of quiet determination rapidly succeeded the previous general despondency.[360]

Chapter 6
• • • • •

Court Martial and Execution

On Monday morning, 1 May, the prisoners were assembled in the gymnasium of Richmond barracks for what was essentially an identification parade. They were screened for trial, deportation or release. 'G Men' – detectives from the G Branch political surveillance unit of the Dublin Metropolitan Police – scrutinised the rebels and pinpointed certain individuals. Colbert was one of those whom the detectives specified for closer attention. The leaders were isolated. Before they were taken away, Ceannt 'strode up and down … looking very much like a caged lion. Sean McDermott and Colbert smiled and nodded cheerily across to each one of us in turn'.[361] Their good humour aside, 'they looked very tired and worn out'.[362]

The staff of the 4th Battalion were Commandant Éamonn Ceannt, Vice-Commandant Cathal Brugha, Adjutant Seamus Murphy, Quartermaster Seamus Kenny, and Assistant Quartermaster Phil Cosgrave (the last three having been in Jameson's). There were another half-a-dozen staff officers. All of these men held higher ranks than Colbert. The captains of the other five companies in the battalion held an equal rank to Colbert (these included Adjutant Murphy of A Company and Patrick Pearse of E Company, nominally part of the 4th Battalion but attached primarily to GHQ). Seamus Murphy was in the same batch of prisoners as Colbert and in full uniform, but he was not picked out. There was a very simple and straightforward reason for that – he was not familiar to the G Men:

> The question of Colbert taking Murphy's place does not arise at all, it was just that good luck favoured Murphy and he was deported … Colbert and Murphy did not, and could not, exchange uniforms, as Colbert was a very small sized man and Murphy was very tall and well-built.

In Christy Byrne's opinion, 'Murphy was a very manly fellow and certainly would not shirk facing a court-martial and its sentence had he been picked out for it'. Byrne made the convincing case that

> … what saved Murphy's life was the fact that he was not very prominent before the Rising and was not, as far as I know, known to the police. Against this, Colbert made himself very prominent during the anti-recruiting campaign for the British army that was then in full swing before the Rising. He wore kilts and frequently pulled down Union

Jacks and recruiting posters and helped to break up meetings. He also drilled the Fianna in the open.[363]

The circumstances of the confirmation of Colbert's death
sentence support Byrne's contention.

Britain had customarily deployed martial law in its colonies
when insurrection could not be subdued by troops acting
for the civil administration. It usually involved the establishment of military courts to try and, if expedient, to execute
prisoners. The primary limit to the exercise of power by the
army in these circumstances was no more or less than the
judgment of senior officers. The immediate legal response of
the authorities in Easter week was the declaration of martial
law by the head of the Irish executive, Baron Wimborne, the
Lord Lieutenant and Governor General. The government in
London then revoked the right to ordinary trial for offences
contrary to the Defence of the Realm Act (DORA), and
substituted court martial in its place. General Sir John Maxwell arrived in Ireland on 28 April as 'military governor' of
the country, with 'plenary powers under martial law'. He literally assumed the power of life and death for a spell. That
there existed simultaneously two inconsistent legal regimes
meant that Maxwell was compelled to work under DORA
regulations, but he did so in such a way as to approximate
martial law. In some respects, he devised his own system and
supplanted due process. Thus, the exact legal standing of the
post-Rising courts martial is shrouded with uncertainty.[364]

More to the point, however, is the fact that the rule of law gave way to political exigencies in the aftermath of the Rising, the army and government colluding to protect their interests in a disturbing fashion. More than 3,000 civilians, men and women, were rounded up from all over the country and filtered through Richmond barracks. There is no doubt as to the role of those executed, but the same cannot be said of many of those arrested in the provinces. Nearly 2,000 were deported or interned. This only served as a further spur to radicalisation, and alienated entire communities. Summary Field General Courts Martial were staged for the first 160 prisoners tried. This was a rudimentary form of trial, usually reserved for soldiers on active duty. It offered few rights to the accused, its dominant purpose being to maintain army discipline.

British forces were under intense pressure on the continent, and there were concerns about the extent and dire circumstances of the trials and executions on the western front under the same crude system employed in Ireland. The release of records would have caused severe political embarrassment and damaged British morale, sapping energy from the war effort. Public opinion abroad was also a consideration, especially in America, which was still neutral. Closer to home, the recruiting campaign had to be safeguarded against negative publicity. The secrecy surrounding the process was jealously guarded by the army and government. The trials were held in camera, behind closed doors and away from the public and press. The official transcripts were withheld until the end of the century. The proceedings were swift and perfunctory. After 17 May, when the last death sentence was passed, the few remaining trials were General Courts Martial, which afforded greater protection to the accused.[365]

The army had a typed 'Form for Assembly and Proceeding of Field General Court Martial on Active Service'. It was called upon when 'Ordinary General Court Martial' was 'not practicable', or if the offence was of a serious character.[366] A Field General Court Martial was easier to convene than a General Court Martial. None of the three required officers had to be legally trained, and only the most senior had to hold the rank of captain or higher. A unanimous verdict was necessary to impose a death sentence, which then had to be confirmed by Maxwell, who exercised his power with alarming alacrity.

Ninety death sentences were passed, and fifteen were carried out (Roger Casement was tried for treason before a London jury, and hanged in Pentonville prison on 3 August). The first trials were convened on 2 May, as the cases of Patrick Pearse, Thomas MacDonagh and Tom Clarke were heard. The following day it was the turn of Ned Daly, Willie Pearse, Michael O'Hanrahan and Joseph Plunkett. Éamonn Ceannt's court martial ran over 3 and 4 May. Colbert, along with John MacBride, Seán Heuston and Thomas Kent, was tried on 4 May. Michael Mallin was the sole defendant on 5 May, and the last death sentences to be enforced were handed out to James Connolly and Seán MacDiarmada on 9 May. Most of the cases were heard at Richmond barracks. The exceptions were Casement, Kent (who was tried in Fermoy, County Cork, having killed a policeman nearby) and Connolly, who, owing to his injuries, faced his charges propped up in a bed at the temporary Red Cross hospital in Dublin Castle.

The executions which followed soon began to resemble acts of vengeance more than justice. As well as the accused and the three court-martial officers, each trial was attended by witnesses, detectives and a prosecutor. Lieutenant William G Wylie, Kings Counsel, was appointed as prosecutor with only a few hours notice. Wylie was a member of the Officer Training Corps, a small reservist unit based in Trinity College, and had assisted in suppressing the Rising.[367] A specialist in civil law, he had no experience of courts martial work, but he was fair-minded and courageous.[368] He condemned the haste and secrecy of the proceedings, arguing that the trials should have taken place in public. His proposal that the accused be allowed access to legal representation met with an almost blanket rebuttal, but he did succeed, after the opening trials on 2 May, in ensuring that defendants were permitted to call witnesses if they so wished. However, the only potential friendly witnesses were other prisoners, and events were moving rapidly. The prisoners could speak in their own defence, but their words were not given the weight of sworn testimony and sometimes went unrecorded. When British officer Captain John Bowen-Colthurst was tried for the murders he committed during the Rising, he faced a General Court Martial, which provided him with legal counsel and the protection of a Judge Advocate.[369] The contrast was conspicuous. The rapidity of the whole process was also striking, given that reinforcements from England were turned back as of 30 April and order had been restored while executions continued apace.

The common charge was that the accused

> Did an act to wit did take part in an armed rebellion and in the waging of war against His Majesty the King, such act being of such a nature as to be prejudicial to the Defence of the Realm and being done with the intention and for the purpose of assisting the enemy.

A court martial was prevented from imposing the death penalty, save where the breach of the regulations was carried out with the intention of assisting the enemy, namely Germany.[370] Only Willie Pearse pleaded guilty. Ironically enough, while holding the rank of captain, he was little more than an aide-de-camp – his most serious transgression was being Patrick's brother. The speed of events, the deficiencies in Dublin Castle's intelligence and the volume of suspects meant that little compelling proof was provided. What evidence was produced was often entirely circumstantial and occasionally erroneous and distorted.[371] Connolly and Pearse were primarily concerned with protecting the legacy of the Rising, but others fought their cases. Heuston and Ceannt disputed inaccurate information. Daly was one of those who denied any contact with German forces, and stressed that all he did was for Ireland alone.[372] Mallin adopted the ethically dubious strategy of deceitfully portraying himself as one of the rank and file, and went so far as to hide behind Countess Markievicz.[373]

Colbert was one of those who demonstrated either disdain for the court or what might have been apathy. Only one witness testified against him, namely Major James A Armstrong of the Royal Inniskilling Fusiliers, an Irishman home on leave from the western front. He was present at Jacob's during one of the last engagements of the Rising. The South Staffordshires anticipated taking the surrender of the garrison, but some of the rebels, perhaps unaware of the situation or simply wishing to fight on, inflicted casualties on the soldiers. This incident formed the basis of all the evidence he gave at a number of courts martial. Armstrong was later in command of the troops at St Patrick's Park, and took the surrender of four hundred rebels from Jacob's, the South Dublin Union and Marrowbone Lane. Unsurprisingly, he knew practically nothing about Colbert.[374] This mattered little in what was in some respects a show trial, the outcome being almost a foregone conclusion: of the thirty-six prisoners tried at Richmond that day, thirty were sentenced to death.[375] On 11 May, Maxwell sent Prime Minister Asquith a memorandum entitled 'A Short History of rebels on whom it has been necessary to inflict the supreme penalty'. He justified the instances in which he had confirmed the death sentence by citing evidence culled from intelligence sources, as opposed to anything produced by the prosecution.[376]

On the morning of Thursday, 4 May, the day of his trial, Colbert remained wary, conscious of the need to protect the men. He was anxious that rebels did not incriminate themselves or others. He approached a group of prisoners who were

> … talking near a door and [made] them go and stand in the centre of the room, telling them that the doors, walls and windows in the place had ears. Con, small and compact in his uniform, said, 'If you were escorted to a lavatory, you were no sooner in until a soldier, who was not one of your guard, would slip in beside you and ask questions about someone who had yet to stand trial'.

One G Man 'became most abusive as he jeered' at Colbert.[377]

Lieutenant Colonel Douglas Sapte only arrived in Ireland on 4 May, but presided over Colbert's hearing, among others. Sapte had no legal training, and little if any experience of capital courts martial. Born in 1869, Sapte enlisted in 1885 and spent decades serving in India and Africa. He had retired in 1914, but was soon recalled.[378] Having done his soldiering in the colonies, it is likely that Sapte considered rebellion a heinous act. The other two officers were Major WR James and Major DB Frew.

Sapte, James, Frew and Major Armstrong were sworn in. Colbert, prisoner number seventy, was tried as 'Concobar O'Colbaird'. He faced the standard charge of 'assisting the enemy', and a second charge of 'attempting to cause disaffection among the civilian population of His Majesty'. There are competing records of what happened at this point. The official trial transcript suggests that Colbert pleaded not guilty, but made no concerted effort to escape the firing squad. The proceedings were brief, probably lasting only a few minutes. Armstrong testified that

> On 30th April 1916 I was present at Bride Street and Patrick's Park where the British Troops were fired upon. The accused was one of a party which surrendered about 5pm. He was dressed in a Volunteer Captain's uniform and was armed. These officers were armed with pistols or revolvers. These men who surrendered came from the direction in which firing had taken place.[379]

This was essentially the same indiscriminate, imprecise and incidental evidence that Armstrong delivered against Ceannt,

MacBride, MacDonagh and O'Hanrahan.[380] British troops
had indeed been fired upon as he described, but the garrison at Marrowbone Lane had hardly seen a British soldier
or fired a shot in anger since Friday. The issue of timing is
also not entirely clear: Bob Holland and Edward O'Neill put
their departure from the distillery at 6.30pm or after.[381] The
Marrowbone Lane contingent arrived with Ceannt's South
Dublin Union group, after the Jacob's men. Armstrong was
not even aware of which outpost Colbert had served in. The
British version is that Colbert declined the opportunity to
make a statement in his defence in response to Armstrong,
simply telling the court 'I have nothing to say'.[382] Ceannt,
MacBride, MacDonagh and O'Hanrahan had all challenged
Armstrong and cross-examined him.[383] A document written by republicans in Lewes prison in England in 1917 and
smuggled out puts forward the scenario that Colbert was not
just a passive presence, that he sought to defend himself and
perhaps hoped to avoid the supreme punishment:

> In the course of his trial he said he could prove he was not
> at Jacob's. The President said it did not matter whether that
> was proved or not. Colbert said 'very well, if you say it does
> not make any difference, I will not call a witness to prove
> it'.[384]

It is not implausible that the court was of the opinion
that if he was an armed Volunteer officer, it did not matter

which garrison he had surrendered from, and also that Colbert was resigned in the face of this indifference to the truth. The creators of this text may have been among those prisoners who crowded outside the two standing courts in the same wing of Richmond barracks, themselves waiting to be tried, or others that Colbert had a chance to discuss his trial with. Aside from his rank, Armstrong's generic contribution revealed little about Colbert's real role in the Rising. Nonetheless, the verdict was 'Guilty. Death.'[385] Probably on the same day, 4 May, Colbert was transferred to Kilmainham, a defunct prison nearby.[386]

Maxwell classified all the cases under three headings:

> (a) Those who signed proclamation on behalf of provisional Government and were also leaders in actual rebellion in Dublin. (b) Those who were in command of rebels actually shooting down troops, police and others. (c) Those whose offence was murder.

He placed Colbert in category (b), along with Daly, MacBride, Mallin, Heuston, Willie Pearse and O'Hanrahan.[387] Maxwell confirmed Colbert's death sentence on 6 May. His rationale, as he later explained it to Asquith, indicated that Colbert was designated for severe treatment due in large part to his pre-Rising activities:

> This man was one of the most active members of the Sinn Féin organisation [this is accurate in the sense that

Na Fianna and the Irish Volunteers, if not the IRB, were among the nationalist bodies grouped together under the 'Sinn Féin' umbrella term by the British authorities, but Colbert was not actually a member of Sinn Féin]. He was a close associate with all the leaders [the veracity of this statement is arguable], and took a prominent part in the organisation of the rebel army in which he held the rank of Captain. He was armed at the time of his surrender and came from the neighbourhood of houses from which heavy firing had taken place earlier in the day.[388]

The final sentence of Maxwell's account was based on unquestioning acceptance of Armstrong's claims, and was so dubious and vague as to be almost meaningless in the context of Colbert's execution. It applied to hundreds of prisoners. The report was based mostly on assertion rather than substantiation. Life and death depended less on evidence and more on the vagaries of the will of the army, as represented by Maxwell. For instance, Éamon de Valera and Thomas Ashe, two more senior officers who had commanded units that inflicted heavy casualties on the British, were tried on the same day as Colbert, but were not executed.[389]

As civilians being tried by court martial, the rebels were in a unique position and were permitted to correspond and to receive visitors. Unlike the other men facing execution, Colbert refused the opportunity to have the company of his people. He wrote an explanation to his sister Lila: 'I felt it would grieve us both too much'. Colbert was informed that his execution would take place at 3.45am on 8 May. Promulgation followed confirmation, and would have involved an officer entering Colbert's cell and formally reading out the findings of the court and the sentence imposed. In response, Colbert penned at least eleven letters to relatives and friends during Sunday, 7 May, bidding them farewell and seeking their prayers.[390] The letters indicate that he approached his passing without regret, that his conviction in the righteousness of his cause and the legitimacy of his actions was intact, and that he was reconciled to his fate. He had taken solace in the opportunity presented him to prepare for death.

Bob Holland was of the opinion that Colbert 'got the death he prayed and wished for … it must have been a happy release … for he had as much as told me so. I was glad he got his wish'.[391] Within the republican tradition, execution by shooting was regarded as an honourable death.

The letters to his family are redolent of love and affection. They are forthright and unpretentious, and are all the more stirring for their absence of sentimentality. He took the time to reassure family friend Maggie Clarke about her brother, who had served with him in Jameson's, and to encourage her to pursue money she was owed. His other earthly anxieties were that his death did not cause too much pain to his siblings, and that they forgive him anything he owed them. He also expressed the hope that he would 'die well', presumably meaning in a courageous and stoic fashion. But his spiritual concerns that God would save his soul were equally pressing.

My dear Lila,

I did not like to call you to this Gaol to see me before I left this world, because I felt it would grieve us both too much, so I am just dropping you a line to ask you to forgive me anything I do owe you & to say 'Goodbye' to you and all my friends and to get you & them to say a prayer for my soul. Perhaps I'd never get the chance of knowing when I was to die again and so I'll try & die well. I received this morning & hope to do so again before I die.

Pray for me, ask Fr. Devine & Fr. Healy & Fr. O'Brien to say a Mass for me also any priests you know.

May God help us – me to die well – you to bear your sorrow.

I am, your loving brother,

Conn.

I send you a prayerbook as a token. Write to Nan, Jack & Willie [sister and brothers in San Francisco] & ask them to pray for me.

My dear Mack,

Just a line to say 'Goodbye' and to ask you pray for me. God has given me the grace to know when I'm to die. May He grant that I die well. Forgive me anything I owe you.

Goodbye,

Your loving brother,

Conn.

My dear Nora,

Just a line to say "Goodbye" to you and yours and ask you to say a prayer for my soul. Don't blame me – perhaps God's way of saving my soul.

Goodbye and God bless you and yours,

I am,

Your loving Brother,

Conn.

My dear Jim,

Don't fret when you see this, believe me I have a good chance of dying well, which may God grant. I'll pray for you all, so also you pray for me,

Goodbye,

I am,

Your loving brother,

Conn.

My dear Gretta,

Forgive the writer for his negligence & want of affection for now he'll not see you again. Say a prayer for his soul, which I hope will soon see heaven where I'll see those who are gone before and where I'll be able to prayer for you.

Don't fret for with God's help I'll die in His Grace.

With much love,

I am,

Your loving brother,

Conn.

My dear Katty,

Goodbye and God bless you,

Forgive me the little I owe you – I would I could ere I died, but 'twas not to be.

Pray for me when I am gone and I hope we'll all meet in Heaven – Give my love to Dick [husband] and the children and remember me.

Ever your fond brother,

Conn.

My dear Aunt Mary [O'Donnell, Tullycrine, County Clare, Colbert's mother's sister],

Just a line to ask you to pray for my soul & to get all your family and friends to do so also.

I am to be shot tomorrow morning at 3.45 a.m. and then God have mercy on me. I'll remember you all in my prayers too and we'll all, with God's Grace, meet in Heaven.

I am,

Your loving nephew,

Conn.

My dear Máire [O'Donnell],

Just a line to ask your prayers for the repose of my soul, which is to depart at 3.45 tomorrow morning.

Get the nuns & all to pray for me – for you know what a sinner I have been [Máire was a nun in France at the time]. May God bless you and all.

I am,

Your loving Cos,

Conn.

My dear Friends [the Dalys of Limerick],

Just a line to say Goodbye & ask your prayers for my poor soul. May God prosper you & yours. May He Save Ireland.

Goodbye

I am

Your firm friend

Conn

My dear Maggie [Clarke],

Just a line to tell you that as far as I know Joe is alright, to ask you to pray for me, and to get all your friends to do so, for ere this reaches you I'll be shot. I hope you got the money from Mr. O'Donnell of Kennedy's, and if not, get it from Mr. Kennedy.

Pray for me,

I am your friend,

Conn.

My dear Annie and Lily [Cooney sisters],

I am giving this to Mrs. Murphy for you [Sheila Murphy, like the Cooneys, was a prisoner in Kilmainham at this time. She was sharing a cell with Lily O'Brennan, who was Áine Ceannt's cousin.[392] Colbert, having got to know Murphy in Jameson's and having seen her at Mass in Kilmainham that morning – and evidently also not wishing to distress either of the Cooneys, who he had also seen at Mass – requested that she be brought to his cell on the night of 7 May, most probably when he had finished writing his letters]. She'll not mind to hear of what is happening and she'll get all of you to pray for those of us who must die. Indeed you girls give us courage, and may God grant you Freedom soon in the fullest sense. You won't see me again, and I feel it better for you not to see me, as you'd only be lonely, but now my soul is gone and pray God it will be pardoned all its crimes.

Tell Christy [Byrne] and all what happened and ask them
to pray for me.

Goodby dear friends and remember me in your prayers.

Your fond friend,

C. Ó Colbáird.

Sheila Murphy was not permitted to take this letter with
her before it was censored, and the Cooneys only received
it on the Tuesday, 9 May. Their version of the letter includes
the postscript: 'Mrs. M. will give you Christy's watch'. The
Cooneys were also given possession of Colbert's watch, and
passed it on to Byrne. They gave his prayerbook and some
items of clothing to his sister Lila. He wanted Annie to keep
his rosary beads.[393]

Sheila Murphy's account of her meeting with Colbert on
7 May reveals something of his mental and physical condi-
tion only hours before his execution:[394]

> I met Con Colbert there [in Jameson's]. I did not know
> him before that, only by appearance. ... After the surren-
> der about eighty girls, including myself, were arrested and
> detained in Kilmainham. I saw Con Colbert at Mass on
> Sunday, 7th May, with Eamonn Ceannt, Michael Mallin
> and ... Heuston ... I saw [Colbert and the others] going
> to Holy Communion ... We were in the gallery and we
> saluted the men as they passed out.
>
> On that Sunday night, when I was in my cell with another

girl [Áine Ceannt's sister, Lily O'Brennan], the sentry came to the door with a wardress and said someone wanted to see me. When I got outside the wardress asked me did I know anyone of the name of Colbert. I said I could not tell until I would see him. I was taken before the Governor who ordered that I be brought to Con Colbert. There was a soldier present during our interview. When I entered the cell Con was lying on the floor with a blanket over him. There was no plank bed or mattress of any kind in the cell and the night was bitterly cold. There was a little table and stool in the cell and a candle lighting on the table as Con was expecting the priest. He jumped up when he saw me and said: 'How are you? I am one of the lucky ones.' Of course I knew what was going to happen to him when he said that. 'I am proud', he said, 'to die for such a cause. I will be passing away at the dawning of the day'. I said: 'What about Eamonn Ceannt?' He was the only other one of the men I knew. He replied: 'He has drawn the lucky lot as well'.

Con had his prayer-book with him and said he would leave it to his sister, Lila. 'Here', he said, 'is what I am leaving you,' and he took three buttons belonging to his Volunteer uniform out of his pocket. 'They left me nothing else', he added. He appeared to be happy and said he was quite resigned to go before his Maker. He said he never felt happier as he never thought he would get the honour of dying for Ireland. I said to him that he was setting an example for all soldiers of the way they should die. The soldier who was present was crying. He said: 'If only we could die such deaths'. I asked Con why he did not send for his sister, Lila. He said that he did not like to cause trouble. I said: 'Never mind the trouble; they are bound to send for her.' He said that she might find it hard to bear the strain.

I knelt down and asked him for his blessing. He gave it to me and said in a simple earnest way: 'We will all meet above under happier circumstances.' He asked me when I heard the volleys fired on the following morning at Ceannt, Mallin and himself [this might suggest he did not know Heuston was to be executed also] would I say a Hail Mary for their departing souls. I said: 'Of course I will'. 'If you are let down to exercise tomorrow', he added, 'and if you meet all the girls ask them to say one Hail Mary each for the three of us who will be gone'. I promised to carry out his request. When leaving him I said to him that a martyr's death was a noble one. He was smiling as I was going out and said: 'The priest will be here in a minute now so I will not lie down again'. I heard the volleys fired the next morning at break of day and myself and the girl who was sleeping in the cell with me got up and we said the De Profundis three times for the men who were passing into eternity.

Colbert was executed in the stonebreakers' yard at 3.45am, or a little after. The firing party of twelve soldiers with Lee Enfields, supervised by a non-commissioned officer and commanded by an officer, was assembled at army headquarters at the nearby Royal Hospital and marched to the gaol, where the rifles were loaded out of their sight. The prisoner was brought from his cell to a central passageway. He was blindfolded and his wrists were tied. The medical officer, in Colbert's case Captain Stanley of the Royal Army Medical Corps, placed a small white card to mark his heart and provide a clear target. He was then walked to the yard. The firing squad was lined up at only ten paces from the subject, a distance from which a volley of rifle fire could inflict catastrophic injuries but not necessarily kill.

Those selected for firing parties were often reluctant to participate, disinclined to cut down an unarmed man. One bullet may have been a blank or 'conscience' round, so that no member of the squad could be certain whether he had personally shot the prisoner or not. This fortified all members to discharge their weapon and to aim true. Encouragement may not have been necessary in Dublin in 1916, however; all of the executions were performed by the Sherwood Foresters, who had taken grievous losses. As against this, the soldiers were mainly raw conscripts. Major CH Heathcote oversaw most of the executions, including Colbert's. He had been commissioned in the Foresters in 1897, and served in the regular army until 1907. Returning to civilian life as an architect, he remained part of the territorial reserve and resumed full-time service in August 1914.[395]

How efficiently the executions were conducted is open to question. There are two first-hand accounts relating to 8 May. One is from Rose McNamara, who was being held in Kilmainham. Her diary entry for the day read: 'Loud reports of shots at daybreak. We say prayers for, whoever it was; heard terrible moans; then a small shot; then silence.'[396] The 'small shot' would have been the officer in charge of a firing squad administering the *coup de grâce* by handgun. Second Lieutenant AA Dickson commanded a firing squad, and recorded that after a single volley, 'the rebel dropped to the ground like an empty sack':

> I was glad there was no doubt the rifles had done their work and there was no need for me to do what the old Major had told me, about the officer going back and finishing the job with his revolver.

Given that there were four executions on 8 May, these accounts are not necessarily contradictory. However, Captain Stanley, the medical officer present at the executions, later admitted that 'the rifles of the firing party were waving like a field of corn'. He asked to be excused attendance at further executions.[397] Colbert's death certificate might have been revealing, but, as army procedure dictated, it is not part of his court martial record.[398] Neither are those of Ceannt, Heuston or Mallin, the others shot on 8 May. In fact, the death certificates of most of the executed men are missing from their trial files. The certificates are referred to in some of the records, so they must have been removed at a later point.[399] This may have been for administrative purposes. It seems more likely, however, that it was done to conceal information, perhaps that executions were botched and did not deliver the army's expected standard of instantaneous death. A public admission of this nature would have caused huge discomfiture.

Colbert's body, together with those of Ceannt, Heuston and Mallin, was immediately transported by horse-drawn ambulance to Arbour Hill military prison cemetery. After the chaplain carried out a short funeral service, he was buried without a coffin, in quicklime, alongside the other executed men in a trench in an exercise yard that constituted their common grave. The manner of the interments was controversial. There were claims that the British had denied the men a Christian burial, and controversy over whether the ground was consecrated or not. Colbert was laid to rest between MacBride and Ceannt.[400]

The front page of the *Evening Herald* of 31 May, under the heading 'Last Moments of Volunteer Leader', described how Colbert

> … died joking the men who were preparing him for death … When one of the soldiers was fixing the white cloth on his breast to indicate his heart he told them 'his heart was far away at the moment'.

Father Augustine, who accompanied Colbert to his execution, felt compelled to submit a response to this 'quite inaccurate and fanciful' account:

> I owe it to his memory to give the true one. There was no joking, not even the semblance of it. Poor Colbert was far too beautiful and too reverent a character to joke with anyone in such a solemn hour. I know very well where his heart was then. It was very near to God and to the friends he loved. What really happened was this. While my left arm linked the prisoner's right, and while I was whispering something in his ear, a soldier approached to fit a a bit of paper on his breast. While this was being done, he looked down, and addressing the soldier in a perfectly cool and natural way said: 'Wouldn't it be better to pin it up higher – nearer the heart?' The soldier said something in reply, and then added: 'Give me your hand now'. The prisoner seemed confused and extended his left hand. 'Not that', said the soldier, 'but the right. The right was accordingly extended, and having shaken it warmly, the kindly human hearted soldier proceeded to bind gently the prisoner's hands behind his back, and afterwards blindfolded him. Some minutes later, my arm still linked in his, and accompanied by another priest, we entered the dark corridor leading to the yard and, his lips moving in prayer, the brave lad went forth to die.[401]

Augustine's description dwells on the spiritual rather than the prurient, and probably takes into account the feelings of Colbert's family, but it is less illuminating for that.

Colbert's case was raised in the House of Commons at Westminster. PJ O'Shaughnessy, MP for West Limerick, questioned

> ... what grounds there were for [his] execution ... whether his youthful age was taken into account before sentence, whether he was a signatory of the Republican Proclamation, and whether he had the ministration of a priest before death?

Mr HJ Tennant, the Under Secretary of State for War, replied that 'Colbert was a captain in the rebel army. Every circumstance connected with the case including that mentioned by the honourable member was given due consideration before the sentence of death was confirmed.' He confirmed that 'Colbert was not a signatory of the Republican Proclamation, the ministration of a priest was given in his case, as in others, before the sentence was carried out.'[402]

Amidst the fog of war that descended during the Rising, and lingered in its immediate aftermath, Lila Colbert had to rely on others for information about her brother. And because Con did not contact her, she was at work on 8 May, ignorant of his execution: 'when the news was announced in the Stop Press, the other girls [at Lafayette's] kept it from her

and later broke the news to her as gently as they could'.[403]
Many others were in a similar situation, having seen a loved
one killed or deported.

Groups sympathetic to those distressed financially made
instantaneous efforts to raise and distribute aid. Within a
week of the last executions, the Irish National Aid Association was established, 'to effect cooperation amongst four different Committees which had been formed to relieve those
who had suffered as a result of the rising of the previous
month'.[404] It involved members of the Irish Parliamentary
Party. The Irish Volunteer Dependants' Fund, founded by
Áine Ceannt and Kathleen Clarke during the first week of
May and dominated by women relatives of the executed
men, was another autonomous body working in the same
field. Such duplication was self-defeating and in August, after
some mutual suspicions had been overcome and a compromise brokered, the National Aid Association and the Volunteer Dependants' Fund merged, to form the unimaginatively
titled Irish National Aid and Volunteer Dependants' Fund:

> The objects of the Association are to make adequate provi-
> sion for the families and dependants of the men who were
> executed, of those who fell in action, and of those who were
> sentenced to penal servitude in connection with the Insur-
> rection of Easter, 1916; And, in addition, to provide for the
> necessities of those others who suffered by reason of par-
> ticipation or suspicion of participation in the Insurrection.

Employment was to be arranged for those who had lost jobs as a result of involvement, real or imagined, in the rebellion.[405] The Association also set about determining the financial circumstances of the families and dependants of the executed men and those killed in action. It listed their income, both prior to and after the rebellion, aid already received, the dependants' suggestions, the relevant sub-committee's comments and the recommended grant. The suggested sums were approved by the executive on 10 December, but it was unanimously agreed that these amounts 'should be regarded as the minimum, with the possibility of increase later on if the funds permitted'.[406] The assessment document emphasised the significant differences in the circumstances of the executed men. Middle-class Thomas MacDonagh's prior income was over £350, and Éamonn Ceannt's £220 (and the wealthier the family or the higher their social class, the more relief they received). Colbert's paltry income had been 'Just sufficient for himself'. He had been listed as having 'no dependants', but his 'delicate sister' who 'lives on the home farm with her brother' received £150 from the American Relief Fund.[407] The 'delicate sister' was probably Gretta, who died in January 1919 and was buried in Templeathea with her parents.

In subsequent decades, Mack, Bridget and Lila Colbert applied as dependants of Con's for awards from the state under a series of Army Pension Acts that related to military service during the 1916–23 period.[408] If there was a hierarchy of the martyrs of the campaign for independence, Colbert was surely near the top. His siblings were not afforded special treatment, however, and had to follow the standard procedures (despite arguments in their favour from prominent public figures). Their name did not translate into automatic entitlement. Neither did it guarantee eventual success.

In late 1937, in a formal submission to the Minister for Defence, Frank Aiken, Mack set out the reasons for his claim:

> In 1916 the racing authorities & the racing community in general were decidely anti-Sinn Féin & made racing so impossible for me that my profession as a jocky became practically useless, as a matter of fact on a very trivial point they sought satisfaction & disqualified me from racing for 12 months. Not only did I suffer in my profession as a jocky, but also being the owner of the Colbert home, it was an open house for all men on the run. The Black & Tans raided and destroyed more than once leaving me often to claim for compensation which I never did, hoping from year to year to get on my feet, & feeling anything I had lost was in the Nation's cause. Unfortunately my circumstances became worse instead of better … in spite of all my endeavours the Bank sold out Con's R.I.P old home a few months ago.

Mack followed up in early 1938, writing to Dan Breen, TD, 'to ask you to interest yourself on my behalf':

… you know so very well all I suffered for the past 20 years owing to my connection with 1916. As we have our own Irish government in power now, I am sure it will deal with my claim as generously as I gave to the cause. In my claim knowing it would get every attention I did not think it necessary to state that I had seven children all under 15 years, but I mention it now to you, as you will realize what it means to me to try & educate them, so as to get positions in their own country. You know I had hopes many a time of getting on my feet but luck seemed to be against me, leaving me in the unfortunate position of being very much in debt, struggling to pay instalments on my rent & rates. I often think it is strange that God sent me so many disappointments seeing that in 1918 I refused an offer of £3,000 for Con's home, as much as from a National point of view as any other & as you know the bank sold us out a few months ago for a small debt of mine.

Breen asked Aiken 'to do something for him – he is badly in need of it'. The Minister adhered rigidly to the terms of the legislation:

Mr. Colbert does not appear to have been a member of any of the organisations mentioned in the Acts nor does he appear to be an eligible dependant. Consequently I regret that there are no provisions in the Acts under which a claim by him might be considered. There are no funds at my disposal out of which compensation might be paid to Mr. Colbert for loss of employment.

It was not until 1953, prompted by the likelihood of favourable statutory changes, that Brigid and Lila involved themselves in the pensions process. Brigid was 'home on holiday from England and I see by the *Press* that the relatives of the 1916 men (who died for Ireland) are to have a pension'. She hoped that it would enable her 'to spend the latter part of my life in Ireland'. Donnchadh Ó Briain, Fianna Fáil TD for West Limerick, made represeantions to the Minister for Defence, Oscar Traynor, regarding Lila's case: she lived with Con and 'kept house for him'. Brigid did not pursue her claim at this point, but Lila, sometimes grudgingly, engaged with the scheme. A civil servant, Lila had reached the retirement age of sixty-five in 1952, but was retained as a Health Visitor by the Department of Social Welfare. Ó Briain contacted Traynor again at the end of 1953, to relay 'a bitter complaint' from Lila:

She was visited by a lady investigations officer from the S.W. [Social Welfare] Dept and she regarded the whole thing as a terrible inquisition. The officer had a form containing a long series of questions of a most detailed character. I explained that such was normal procedure in regard to these applications but I feel at the same time that in the case of applications from relatives of Easter Week men that the investigation need not be so searching or so humiliating.

He hoped that the Social Welfare Department would 'be more careful of susceptibilities of feelings' and suggested that 'the relatives of the Easter Week men are in a class apart. I feel that the grant of pensions in these cases should be made as easy as possible'. Lila had not been dependent on Con at the time of his death. In fact, 'deceased just contributed towards his own keep', according to an official note in her file. She now lived alone in a rented flat, and did not wish to disclose her earnings as parts of a means test. But it was now possible to consider factors such as age, physical infirmity and financial circumstances when assessing requests, and Traynor used the discretionary powers available to him to recommend an annuity of £125 per annum.

Only one allowance in respect of the same deceased person could be paid at any one time, and this may have been a factor in Brigid's disconnection. In 1957, however, her case was taken up by Sister Mary Columba, who, in light of Brigid's 'present difficulty' (unemployment), had secured her a position as a housekeeper to a community of priests near Bristol:

I feel that she should be able to settle down in Ireland in her old age and not be looking for public assistance in a cold place like Bristol. She does not know that I am writing

... Anyone who has had any connection with Easter Week should get a wee bit of consideration I think.

Brigid would become eligible for a stipend if Lila pre-deceased her. The regulations had changed again before Ó Briain revisited her case in 1963, however. Brigid had been nursing in England since 1915, and so was not depend-ent on Con in 1916. Nonetheless, her case was judged to merit £158 per annum initially, and this quickly increased to £166. Brigid died on 6 January 1973, and Lila died on 26 November 1974.

Chapter 7

• • • • •

Conclusion

On 4 May 1958, a memorial plaque to Colbert was placed over a bed in Barrington's Hospital, Limerick, donated by Eamon Martin on behalf of Na Fianna Éireann veterans.[409] Dublin, Cork and Limerick Fianna units had assembled in the city for the ceremony. The unveiling was performed by Éamon Dore, who fought in the GPO during the Rising and was married to Nora, one of the Daly sisters. Dore's speech is a classic example of the type of glorification of the 1916 martyrs that was standard in nationalist Ireland. Colbert's spirituality was emphasised, and he was rendered seemingly infallible:

> Small in stature, dressed invariably in breeches and long stockings, when not in Fianna uniform, his sturdy walk made him look much taller than his five or so feet in height. Of tremendous strength and endurance, with an indomitable will, and with his wants pared down to the bare necessaries of life, his money and his time were devoted

wholeheartedly and exclusively to preparing himself and his comrades for the inevitable clash with the country's enemy. He had no time for pettiness nor hate nor defeatism but neither could he see why everybody was not as sincere and earnest as he was. He did not suffer fools, knaves or poltroons gladly and the slavish in spirit were anathema. … Yet in ordinary life he was the humblest of men with no pretensions. He had a fundamental understanding, in nationality as in religion, that was a guiding light to his dedicated life: shame had no place in his being. … His life was one of suppression of self; it was dedicated as truly as if he were a hermit monk. All the longing and striving that are common to the normal man – worldly ambition, a future home and all the both signify – had no place in his scheme of things … no man could be a better example of unselfish work, sense of duty, and the right thing to do at all times.[410]

What is perhaps most remarkable about Dore's tribute, however, is not how inflated it is, but how much truth it contains amid the hyperbole. The focus on altruism, conviction and valour was apposite. It should be matched by consideration of more problematic issues. Colbert's reputation does not need to be transformed, but it does need to be modified.

Colbert's dedication to the pursuit of Irish freedom was absolute, and the staunchness of his belief in its rightfulness did not waver. He gave of himself to an extent and in a fashion that was rare – emotionally, financially, physically and spiritually. The real Colbert is a much more interesting character than the impossibly pure symbol, however. The persistent fiction about his self-sacrifice in favour of his fellow officer Séamus Murphy has sustained the myth but not served the man well. The two must be separated. The focus on his youthfulness denies his pragmatism and shrewdness. His boyish and innocent looks should not disguise his deadly intent and the gravity of his actions. He was without scruples in his recruiting policies and, like many of those he trained, he proved willing to kill and be killed.

While there was much about Colbert that is likeable and admirable, there were a number of contradictions inherent in his behaviour. He was by turns good-humoured and compassionate, quasi-puritanical and ruthless. The rush to sanctify him has made him appear more straight-laced than may have been the case. In personal matters, he was a considerate man. He could be flexible, realistic and tolerant. If his existence was rather Spartan, he was not the only pioneer in the country or the only observer of penitential practices during Lent. He grumbled about the holding of a céilí at Easter, but attended anyway, overcoming his reservations in the service of the cause. He was a pioneer, but his attitude to his sister who struggled with 'uisge beatha' was sympathetic. He did not judge and condemn her. Rather, he encouraged and supported her.

He was not charismatic, but he was an effective and popular leader. Physically, he was small but imposing. His bravery was unquestionable. He did not ask or expect of others everything he was prepared to do himself. He was more concerned about the lives of his men than his own. Initially self-conscious about what he perceived as his limitations, his mentality changed over time as he went from being an insecure young man, lacking confidence in himself and his place in the militant movement, to an influential personality. His acumen and commitment won the esteem and trust of the most senior insurgents. His execution was not an anomaly. His deeds in the years before 1916 represented such a peril to British rule that they ensured he suffered the death penalty after the Rising.

He did not have anything like a rogueish charm, but he must have had some earnest allure about him. There was more than one young republican woman who found Colbert attractive and would have been willing to pursue a courtship with him. In turn, Colbert made affectionate gestures to more than one woman. But he did not develop any relationship beyond that. Whether this was a deliberate decision on his part – to remain single, so as to spare a sweetheart the pain of his likely loss – or just an accident of timing, is impossible to know. Love of country trumped all others for Colbert the patriot.

The most prescient of Éamon Dore's comments was perhaps that 'the slavish in spirit were anathema' to Colbert, and that he found it difficult to understand alternative opinions. He wrote of Robert Emmet being murdered by a combination of 'the brutal Saxon' and his own nation's 'slovenliness'. 'So foolish', in Colbert's words, were the Irish people in the first decade of the twentieth century that they could be abused and led astray by the base turncoats of the Irish Parliamentary Party yet still pledge their allegiance. The tone seems to be equal parts sympathy and disdain for the misguided.

It is possible to discern in Colbert the instincts and elitist streak of one of the self-selected revolutionary vanguard who took it upon themselves not only to construe but to conduct majority public opinion. If they were right to detect an aspiration for full independence when they looked into the hearts and read the minds of their fellow Irish nationalists, it did not make their efforts to force their visions into reality any more democratic.

The Rising, however, must be set in the context of the *á la carte* constitutionalism of the Home Rule crisis. It can be interpreted as a manifestation of the threat of violence that already existed in Irish politics, and hovered ominously between Belfast, Dublin and London. To dismiss Colbert as nothing more than a man of violence would be to do an injustice to him and his ideals. His contribution was psychological as well as military, focusing not only on how to fight for freedom but emphasising the value of ethical citizenship, the Irish capacity for self-government, the right to self-determination and the legitimacy of the claim to independence. As a member of the Gaelic League, the Irish Republican Brotherhood, Na Fianna Éireann and the Irish Volunteers, he performed a vital function in bridging the spectrum between cultural revival, separatist conspiracy and public declaration of force. Republicanism and insurrection, for Colbert, was about the assertion of national sovereignty and liberation from occupation, colonisation and oppression. He projected independent Ireland as a Gaelic utopia. Whether that haven would stand as part of Europe or as an isolated outpost remained to be seen.

Colbert soldiered harmoniously with Catholic, Protestant and dissenter alike. Whatever discord emerged between him and, for instance, Bulmer Hobson, was tactical rather than religious. In his political scorn for TP O'Connor (a Catholic), derided by Colbert as 'only an Irishman in speech and a pro Englisher at heart', there were, however, at least faint resonances of the type of demands for conformity and distrust of difference that were typical of the culturally, socially and doctrinally oppressive sections of Irish society during the later twentieth century. What dispensations he would have made for those who did not subscribe to the vision he espoused, and who traced their lineage through different traditions, is another question that must go unanswered. The capacity that he demonstrated for empathy and compromise in private affairs and in his dealings with Volunteers under his command was at odds with his public and political persona.

It would probably be wishful thinking and demand too great an imaginative leap to suggest that he might have found a way to avoid the errors that his comrades made when in power. There is little chance that he would have favoured a move away from theocracy and the greater separation of Church and State in the first half-century of independence, or more liberal social or economic policies. A more likely scenario is that Colbert himself would have been alienated politically from the Free State that emerged from the revolution.

Bibliography

Archival Sources

Dublin

Allen Library

    Con Colbert Collection

Kilmainham Gaol

    Con Colbert Collection

Military Archives of Ireland

    Bureau of Military History Image Gallery (online access)

    Bureau of Military History Witness Statements (online access)

    Military Service Pensions Collection (online access)

National Archives of Ireland

    1901 Census (online access)

    1911 Census (online access)

National Library of Ireland

    Colonel Joseph Leonard Papers

    Irish National Aid and Volunteer Dependents' Fund Papers

National Museum

    Con Colbert letters

    Irish Volunteer and rebellion notebook (HE EW 1240). Inscription inside front cover: 'Found 4th May '16 in kitchen of S.D.U. – week following Sinn Féin rebellion by David Thompson'

    Duplicate leaf book – includes carbon duplicated script of orders written by Colbert on Easter Monday morning, 1916.

Limerick

University of Limerick Library Special Collections

    Daly Papers

Bibliography

London

National Archives of the United Kingdom

Colonial Office Papers (RIC County Inspectors' and Inspector-General's Reports, CO 904 Papers, are widely available on microfilm under the title 'The British in Ireland, 1914–21')

War Office Papers

Newspapers and Periodicals

An Macaomh

An Scoláire

An Claidheamh Soluis

Bean na hÉireann

Catholic Bulletin

Irish Freedom

Irish Volunteer

Kerryman

Limerick Chronicle

Limerick Leader

National Volunteer

Sinn Féin (daily and weekly editions)

Official Publications

Report of the Royal Commission on the rebellion in Ireland. Minutes of evidence and appendix of documents, H. C., 1916 (Cd. 8311)

Books and Articles

Augusteijn, Joost, 'Motivation: Why did they fight for Ireland? The motivation of Volunteers in the revolution' in Joost Augusteijn (ed.), *The Irish revolution, 1913–23* (London, 2002), pp. 103–20

Augusteijn, Joost, 'The importance of being Irish: Ideas and the Volunteers in Mayo and Tipperary' in David Fitzpatrick (ed.), *Revolution? Ireland, 1917–23* (Dublin, 1990), pp. 25–42

Bateson, Ray, *Memorials of the Easter Rising* (2013)

Barton, Brian, *From behind a closed door: Secret court martial records of the 1916 Easter Rising* (Belfast, 2002)

16 LIVES: CON COLBERT

Bew, Paul, *Ideology and the Irish Question: Ulster unionism and Irish nationalism* (Oxford, 1994)

Brady, Seán, 'Some recollections of 1916 leaders' in *Mungret Annual* (1966), pp. 19–20

Breen, Dan, *My fight for Irish freedom* (Dublin, 1989)

Clarke, Kathleen [Helen Litton (ed.)], *Revolutionary woman: My fight for Ireland's freedom* (Dublin, 1991)

Coldrey, Barry, *Faith and fatherland: The Christian Brothers and the development of Irish nationalism, 1838–1921* (Dublin, 1988)

Collins, Lorcan, *James Connolly* (Dublin, 2012)

Conneely, Mairéad, *Idir dhá chladach / Between two shores: Writing the Aran Islands, 1890–1980* (Oxford, 2011)

Daly, Madge, 'Con Colbert of Athea: Hero and martyr' in Brian Ó Conchubhair (ed.), *Limerick's fighting story, 1916–21: Told by the men who made it* (Cork, 2009), pp. 70–4

Davis, Richard, *Arthur Griffith and non-violent Sinn Féin* (Dublin, 1974)

Dudley Edwards, Ruth, *Patrick Pearse: The triumph of failure* (Dublin, 2006)

Enright, Seán, *Easter Rising 1916: The trials* (Dublin, 2014)

Fitzpatrick, David, 'The geography of Irish nationalism, 1910–21' in *Past and present*, 78 (1978), pp. 113–44

Gifford, Sydney, *The years flew by* (Dublin, 1974)

Hardiman, Adrian, '"Shot in cold blood": Military law and Irish perceptions in the suppression of the 1916 rebellion' in Gabriel Doherty and Dermot Keogh (eds), *1916: The long revolution* (Cork, 2007), pp. 225–49

Hart, Peter, 'The geography of revolutionary violence in Ireland, 1917–23' in *Past and present*, 155 (1997), pp. 142–73

Hay, Marnie, 'Moulding the future: Na Fianna Éireann and its members, 1909–1923' in *Studies, An Irish quarterly review*, 100, 400, pp. 441–54

Hay, Marnie, 'The foundation and development of Na Fianna Éireann, 1909–1916' in *Irish historical studies*, 36, 141 (2008), pp. 53–71

Hay, Marnie, *Bulmer Hobson and the nationalist movement in twentieth-century Ireland* (Manchester, 2008)

Hughes, Brian, *Michael Mallin* (Dublin, 2012)

Hyde, Douglas, *A literary history of Ireland from earliest times to the present day* [originally published 1899] (new edition, London, 1967)

Hynes, Samuel, *A war imagined: The First World War and English culture* (London, 1992)

Laffan, Michael, *The resurrection of Ireland: The Sinn Féin party, 1916–23* (Cambridge, 2005)

Lee, Joe, *Ireland: Politics and society* (Cambridge, 1989)

Lee, Joe, 'The Background: Anglo-Irish relations, 1898–1921', in Cormac O'Malley and Anne Dolan (eds), *'No surrender here!': The Civil War papers of Ernie O'Malley* (Dublin, 2007)

MacGiolla Choille, Breandán (ed.), *Intelligence notes, 1913–16* (Dublin, 1966)

MacLochlainn, Piaras F., *Last words: Letters and statements of the leaders executed after the Rising at Easter 1916* (Dublin, 1990)

Madden, Michael, *Captain Conn Colbert: Defender Watkins' Brewery Marrow Bone Lane Area, Easter Rebellion 1916* (Limerick, 1983)

McGarry, Fearghal, *The Rising. Ireland: Easter 1916* (Oxford, 2010)

Miller, David W., *Church, state and nation in Ireland, 1898–1921* (Dublin, 1973)

Monteith, Robert, *Casement's last adventure* (Dublin, 1953)

Ó Se, Donnchadh, 'Na Fianna Éireann, 1909–1975, with notes on Provisional Fianna Éireann and its offshoots' (unpublished script, courtesy of Pádraig Óg Ó Ruairc)

O'Callaghan, John, 'The Limerick Volunteers and 1916' in Ruán O'Donnell (ed.), *The impact of the 1916 Rising. Among the nations* (Dublin, 2008)

O'Callaghan, John, *Revolutionary Limerick: The republican campaign for independence in Limerick, 1913–21* (Dublin, 2010)

Pearse, Patrick, *Collected works of Pádraic H. Pearse – political writings and speeches* (Dublin, 1924)

Phoenix, Eamon, 'Northern nationalists, Ulster unionists and the development of partition, 1900–21' in Peter Collins (ed.), *Nationalism and unionism: Conflict in Ireland, 1885–1921* (Belfast, 1996), pp. 107–22

Regan, John, *Myth and the Irish state* (Dublin, 2014)

Reilly, Eileen, 'Women and voluntary war work' in Adrian Gregory and Senia Paseta (eds), *Ireland and the Great War: 'A war to unite us all'?* (Manchester, 2002), pp. 49–72

Ryan, Desmond, *The Rising: The complete story of Easter week* (Dublin, 1949)

Sisson, Elaine, *Pearse's patriots: St. Enda's and the cult of boyhood* (Cork, 2004)

Townshend, Charles, *Easter 1916: The Irish rebellion* (London, 2005)

Turpin, John, 'Oliver Sheppard, Albert Power and State Sculptural Commissions' in *Dublin historical record*, 55, 1 (2002), pp. 43–6

White, Lawrence William, 'Cornelius Colbert' in *Dictionary of Irish biography*

Notes

Introduction

1 See Eamon Phoenix, 'Northern nationalists, Ulster unionists and the development of partition, 1900-21' in Peter Collins (ed.), *Nationalism and unionism: conflict in Ireland, 1885-1921* (Belfast, 1996), pp. 107-22.

2 See John Regan, *Myth and the Irish state* (Dublin, 2014).

3 Joe Lee, 'The Background: Anglo-Irish relations, 1898–1921', in Cormac O'Malley and Anne Dolan (eds), *'No surrender here!':The Civil War papers of Ernie O'Malley* (Dublin, 2007).

4 Kilmainham Gaol collection, 7MS-B33-01.

5 Con Colbert to John Colbert, 6 February 1909. Thanks to John Colbert, grand-nephew of Con and grandson of the recipient of this letter, for making the family correspondence available. Thanks also to Lorcan Collins. The letters Con Colbert wrote to John Colbert in San Francisco on 6 February 1909, 9 December 1909, and December 1911 are held in Kilmainham Gaol (13LR-1D44-4).

6 Joseph Lawless, Bureau of Military History Witness Statement [BMH WS] 1043. Lawless, an army officer, happened to be a member of the investigating staff of the Bureau.

7 Gary Holohan, BMH WS 328.

8 Oliver Snoddy pinpointed 23 November as Colbert's start date. See lecture by Oliver Snoddy, History Section, National Museum of Ireland, delivered at the Enterprise Hall, Athea, Sunday 12 December 1965, Appendix C in Michael Madden, *Captain Conn Colbert. Defender Watkins' Brewery Marrow Bone Lane Area, Easter Rebellion 1916* (Limerick, 1983); according to Elaine Sisson, 'Colbert had joined the school as the physical fitness master in the autumn of 1910 and he gave his first lessons in 'military foot drill' and code-signalling that November'. Elaine Sisson, *Pearse's patriots: St. Enda's and the cult of boyhood* (Cork, 2004), p.126.

9 *Limerick Leader*, 5 May 1958; Madge Daly, 'Con Colbert of Athea. Hero and martyr' in Brian Ó Conchubhair (ed.), *Limerick's fighting story, 1916-21: Told by the men who made it* (Cork, 2009), p.70.

10 *An Macaomh*, ii, 2 (May 1913).

11 *An Scoláire*, i, 7 (24 May 1913).

12 Thomas Doyle, BMH WS 168.

13 Quoted in David W. Miller, *Church, state and nation in Ireland, 1898-1921* (Dublin, 1973), pp. 340-1.

14 Seán Prendergast, BMH WS 755.

15 *Catholic Bulletin*, vi, 7 (July 1916), pp. 402-5.

16 Lila Colbert, BMH WS 856.

17 Daly, 'Con Colbert'.

Chapter 1

18 Lawrence William White, *Dictionary of Irish biography*.

19 Colbert, BMH WS 856; Maighréad McGrath, 'Con Colbert', Appendix B in Madden, *Captain Conn Colbert*.

20 Madden, *Captain Conn Colbert*.

21 Con Colbert to John Colbert, 9 February 1909.

22 Daily summaries, 13 October 1920 (National Archives of England, Colonial Office 904/143).

23 Colbert, BMH WS 856; McGrath, 'Con Colbert'; Snoddy lecture.

24 Joseph Clarke, Military Service Pension File (MSP) 24A1135.

25 Colbert, BMH WS 856.

26 Colbert, BMH WS 856.

27 Bob Holland, BMH WS 280.

28 Daly, 'Con Colbert', p.70.

29 Daly, 'Con Colbert', pp 70, 72.

30 Snoddy lecture.

31 Con Colbert to John Colbert, 9 December 1909.

32 David Fitzpatrick, 'The geography of Irish nationalism, 1910-21' in *Past and present*, 78 (1978), p.113.

33 Barry Coldrey, *Faith and fatherland: The Christian Brothers and the development of Irish nationalism, 1838-1921* (Dublin, 1988), p.253.

34 Peter Hart, 'The geography of revolutionary violence in Ireland, 1917-23' in *Past and Present*, 155 (1997), pp. 170-1; Coldrey, *Faith and fatherland*, p.248.

35 Fearghal McGarry, *The Rising. Ireland: Easter 1916* (Oxford, 2010), pp. 38-9, 41.

36 Joost Augusteijn, 'The importance of being Irish. Ideas and the Volunteers in Mayo and Tipperary' in David Fitzpatrick (ed.), *Revolution? Ireland, 1917–23* (Dublin, 1990), pp. 25-7; Joost Augusteijn, 'Motivation: Why did they fight for Ireland? The motivation

ofVolunteers in the revolution' in Joost Augusteijn (ed.), *The Irish revolution, 1913–23* (London, 2002), pp. 115-7.

37 John O'Callaghan, *Revolutionary Limerick: The republican campaign for independence in Limerick, 1913–21* (Dublin, 2010), pp. 23–5.

Chapter 2

38 McGarry, *The Rising*, p.25.

39 Colbert, BMH WS 856.

40 Holohan, BMH WS 328.

41 Prendergast, BMH WS 755.

42 Seán Kennedy, BMH WS 842.

43 Sisson, *Pearse's patriots*, pp. 126-7.

44 Ellen Sarah Bushell, MSP 34REF22326. Bushell served as a courier for Colbert during the Rising.

45 Kilmainham Gaol collection, 7MS-B33-01.

46 Christy Byrne, BMH WS 167; Holland, BMH WS 280.

47 Holohan, BMH WS 328.

48 See, for example, Douglas Hyde, *A literary history of Ireland from earliest times to the present day* [originally published 1899] (new edition, London, 1967), p.630.

49 Mairéad Conneely, *Idir dhá chladach / Between two shores: Writing the Aran Islands, 1890–1980* (Oxford, 2011).

50 Snoddy lecture.

51 'Away From Home' in Kilmainham Gaol collection, 7MS-B33-01.

52 Catríona Crowe (ed.), *Dublin 1911* (Dublin, 2011).

53 Eileen Reilly, 'Women and voluntary war work' in Adrian Gregory and Senia Paseta (eds), *Ireland and the Great War: 'A war to unite us all'?* (Manchester, 2002), p.51.

54 Kilmainham Gaol collection, 7MS-B33-01.

55 Kilmainham Gaol collection, 7MS-B33-01.

Chapter 3

56 Marnie Hay, *Bulmer Hobson and the nationalist movement in twentieth-century Ireland* (Manchester, 2008); 'The foundation and development of Na Fianna Éireann, 1909–1916' in *Irish Historical Studies*, 36, 141 (2008), p.69.

57 Bulmer Hobson, BMH WS 31.

58 *Irish Volunteer*, 28 March, 30 May, 24 October 1914.

59 Liam Brady, BMH WS 676.

60 Thomas Dwyer, BMH WS 1198.

61 Roger McCorley, BMH WS 389.

62 Pounch, BMH WS 267.

63 Seamus MacCaisin, BMH WS 8.

64 Holohan, BMH WS 328.

65 Martin, BMH WS 591; MacCaisin, BMH WS 8.

66 Séamus Reader, BMH WS 627.

67 Prendergast, BMH WS 755.

68 Donnchadh Ó Sé, 'Na Fianna Éireann, 1909–1975, with notes on Provisional Fianna Éireann and its offshoots' (unpublished script, courtesy of Pádraig Óg Ó Ruairc); Colbert, BMH WS 856; Seamus Pounch, BMH WS 267.

69 Patrick Pearse, 'The murder machine' in *Collected works of Pádraic H. Pearse – political-writings and speeches* (Dublin, 1924), p.6.

70 Ruth Dudley Edwards, *Patrick Pearse: The triumph of failure* (Dublin, 2006), pp. 217, 245.

71 Samuel Hynes, *A War imagined: The First World War and English culture* (London, 1992), p.110.

72 Hay, 'The foundation and development of Na Fianna Éireann', pp. 53–71; Marnie Hay, 'Moulding the future: Na Fianna Éireann and its members, 1909–1923' in *Studies, An Irish Quarterly Review*, 100, 400, pp. 441–54.

73 Sisson, *Pearse's patriots*, pp. 120–1.

74 White, *Dictionary of Irish biography*.

75 Holland, BMH WS 280.

76 Tom Young, BMH WS 531.

77 Holland, BMH WS 280.

78 Hay, 'The foundation and development of Na Fianna Éireann', p.54; Hay, 'Moulding the future', p.444.

79 Holland, BMH WS 280.

80 Snoddy lecture.

81 Prendergast, BMH WS 755.

82 Madden, *Captain Conn Colbert*.

83 Ó Sé, 'Na Fianna Éireann'; Patrick Ward, BMH WS 1140.

84 Bob Holland, BMH WS 280.

85 Prendergast, BMH WS 755.

86 White, *Dictionary of Irish biography*; Ó Sé, 'Na Fianna Éireann'.

87 Seán O'Neill, BMH WS 1219.

88 Colbert, BMH WS 856.

89 Seán Brady, 'Some recollections of 1916 leaders' in *Mungret Annual*, 1966, pp. 19–20.

90 Colbert, BMH WS 856.

91 Anna Fahy, BMH WS 202.

92 Brady, 'Some recollections of 1916 leaders', pp. 19–20.

93 Snoddy lecture.

94 Daly, 'Con Colbert', p.72.

95 Holland, BMH WS 280.

96 Pounch, BMH WS 267.

97 Byrne, BMH WS 167.

98 Brady, 'Some recollections of 1916 leaders', pp. 19–20.

99 Holohan, BMH WS 328; Prendergast, BMH WS 755.

100 Colbert, BMH WS 856.

101 Con Colbert to John Colbert, 6 February 1909.

102 Pounch, BMH WS 267.

103 William Christian, BMH WS 646.

104 Seamus Kavanagh, BMH WS 1670.

105 Pounch, BMH WS 267; Ó Sé, 'Na Fianna Éireann'.

106 MacCaisin, BMH WS 8.

107 Michael Lonergan, BMH WS 140.

108 Holohan, BMH WS 328.

109 Hay, 'The foundation and development of Na Fianna Éireann', p.58.

110 MacCaisin, BMH WS 8.

111 *Sinn Féin*, 21 August 1909.

112 *Sinn Féin*, 28 August 1909; Richard Davis, *Arthur Griffith and non-violent Sinn Féin* (Dublin, 1974), pp. 81–3; Michael Laffan, *The resurrection of Ireland: The Sinn Féin party, 1916–23* (Cambridge, 2005), p.30.

113 RIC Inspector-General's Monthly Report [IG], July 1915, Colonial Office [CO]904/97.

114 O'Callaghan, *Revolutionary Limerick*, p.54.

115 *An Claidheamh Soluis*, 21 August 1909.

116 Kavanagh, BMH WS 1670.

117 *Bean na hÉireann*, September 1909. *Bean na hÉireann* (Woman of Ireland) was the newspaper of Inghinidhe na hÉireann (Daughters of Ireland). It ran from 1908 to 1911.

118 Kavanagh, BMH WS 1670.

119 *Irish Freedom*, December 1910.

120 Quoted in Ó Sé, 'Na Fianna Éireann'.

121 Bob Holland, quoted in Ó Sé, 'Na Fianna Éireann'.

122 Alfred White, BMH WS 1207; Ó Sé, 'Na Fianna Éireann'.

123 Eamon Martin, BMH WS 591.

124 Pounch, BMH WS 267.

125 Snoddy lecture.

126 Holohan, BMH WS 328.

127 Sydney Gifford, *The years flew by* (Dublin, 1974), p.57.

128 Ó Sé, 'Na Fianna Éireann'.

129 Desmond Ryan, BMH WS 725.

130 Sisson, *Pearse's Patriots*, p.155; Snoddy lecture.

131 *Irish Freedom*, September 1911, August 1912.

132 Hay, 'The foundation and development of Na Fianna Éireann', p.60.

133 Art O'Donnell, BMH WS 1322.

134 Holohan, BMH WS 328.

135 Ó Sé, 'Na Fianna Éireann'.

136 Snoddy lecture.

137 Pounch, BMH WS 267.

138 Martin, BMH WS 591.

139 Ward, BMH WS 1140.

140 Hobson, BMH WS 31.

141 Byrne, BMH WS 167.

142 Donal O'Hannigan, BMH WS 161; Peter Galligan, BMH WS 170.

143 Martin, BMH WS 591.

Chapter 4

144 For alternative interpretations, see Joe Lee, *Ireland: Politics and society, 1912–85* (Cambridge, 1989), pp. 1–11; and Paul Bew, *Ideology and the Irish Question: Ulster unionism and Irish nationalism, 1912–16* (Oxford, 1994)

145 Kilmainham Gaol collection, 7MS-B33-01.

146 Pearse, 'From a hermitage' in *Collected works*, p.185.

147 Martin, BMH WS 591; Holohan, BMH WS 328; Hobson, BMH WS 31.

148 McGarry, *The Rising*, pp. 72–3.

149 IG, May 1914, Colonial Office 904/93.

150 Seán Fitzgibbon, BMH WS 130.

151 F.X. Martin (ed.), *The Irish Volunteers, 1913–15* (Dublin, 1963), p.144.

152 O'Callaghan, *Revolutionary Limerick*, pp. 25–7.

153 Collins, *James Connolly*, pp. 304–5; Lorcan Collins, *James Connolly* (Dublin, 2012), pp. 304–5.

154 O'Callaghan, *Revolutionary Limerick*, pp. 16, 18, 27–8.

155 Pearse to Daly, 29 January 1914, in Louis le Roux's unpublished biography of John Daly, 'The life and letters of John Daly', chapter 13, p.4 (University of Limerick Library Special Collections, Daly Papers [ULSC, DP] Box 3, Folder 73).

156 Desmond Ryan, *The Rising: The complete story of Easter week* (Dublin, 1949), p.83.

157 Martin, BMH WS 591.

158 Hobson, BMH WS 31.

159 Thomas Doyle, BMH WS 186; Byrne, BMH WS 167.

160 Collins, *James Connolly*, p.246.

161 Doyle, BMH WS 186.

162 Edward O'Neill, BMH WS 203; Holland, BMH WS 280; Doyle, BMH WS 186; Byrne, BMH WS 167.

163 Holland, BMH WS 280; Byrne, BMH WS 167.

164 O'Neill, BMH WS 203.

165 Snoddy lecture.

166 *Irish Volunteer*, 15 May 1915.

167 Précis of Information received by the Crime Branch Special, June 1915, CO 904/97

168 O'Callaghan, *Revolutionary Limerick*, p.38.

169 Holland, BMH WS 280.

170 O'Callaghan, *Revolutionary Limerick*, pp. 204–5.

171 *Irish Freedom*, February 1914.

172 Hay, 'The foundation and development of Na Fianna Éireann', p.63.

173 Pearse, 'To the boys of Ireland' in *Collected works*, pp. 112–23.

174 Helena Molony, BMH WS 391.

175 Holohan, BMH WS328.

176 Kavanagh, BMH WS 1670; Snoddy lecture.

177 Pounch, BMH WS 267.

178 Tom Clarke to John Daly, 26 December 1912 (ULSC, DP, Box 2, Folder 47).

179 IG, May 1912, CO 904/87.

180 Madge Daly memoirs (unpublished), p.85 (ULSC, DP, Box 3, Folder 77).

181 Daly, 'Con Colbert', p.72.

182 Con Colbert to John Daly, 22 August 1913 (ULSC, DP, Box 2, Folder 48).

183 *Irish Volunteer*, 20 February 1915.

184 Kavanagh, BMH WS 208; see also Charles O'Grady, BMH WS 282.

185 Robert Monteith, *Casement's last adventure* (Dublin, 1953), pp. 39, 50–3, 198; MDM, pp. 53–5 (ULSC, DP, Box 3, Folder 77).

186 IG, May 1915; Precis of Information received by the CBS, May 1915, CO 904/97; CBS 'Personality File' on Con Collins, CO 904/192/62; Breandán MacGiolla Choille (ed.), *Intelligence notes, 1913–16* (Dublin, 1966), p.222; Ó Sé, 'Na Fianna Éireann'.

187 *Irish Volunteer*, 5 June 1915.

188 Quirke, 'My life and times', p.6.

189 Holland, BMH WS 280.

190 Dan Breen, *My fight for Irish freedom* (Dublin, 1989), p.14.

191 *National Volunteer,* 29 May 1915; *Limerick Leader*, 26 May 1915; *Irish Volunteer*, 29 May, 5 June 1915; MDM, pp. 87–9 (ULSC, DP, Box 3, Folder 77); Alphonsus O'Halloran, BMH WS 1700.

192 *Limerick Leader*, 10 September 1915.

193 Michael Hartney, BMH WS 1415.

194 *Limerick Chronicle*, 25 May 1915; See also Liam Manahan, BMH WS 456.

195 Patrick Pearse to Madge Daly, 28 May 1915 (ULSC, DP, Box 1, Folder 29).

196 Holland, BMH WS 280.

197 Martin, BMH WS 591.

198 Holohan, BMH WS 328.

199 Ó Sé, 'Na Fianna Éireann'.

200 Martin, BMH WS 591.

201 Martin, BMH WS 591.

202 Hay, 'The foundation and development of Na Fianna Éireann', p.67.

203 Snoddy lecture; Ó Sé, 'Na Fianna Éireann'.

204 Hay, 'The foundation and development of Na Fianna Éireann', pp. 67–8.

205 *Report of the Royal Commission on the rebellion in Ireland. Minutes of evidence and appendix of documents*, H. C., 1916 (Cd. 8311), p.1.

206 O'Callaghan, *Revolutionary Limerick*, pp. 41–2.

207 Daly, 'Con Colbert', pp. 71–2.

208 Brian Barton, *From behind a closed door: Secret court martial records of the 1916 Easter Rising* (Belfast, 2002), p.243.

209 O'Donnell, BMH WS 1322.

210 Snoddy lecture.

211 *The Kerryman*, 23 April 1966; Snoddy lecture; Ó Sé, 'Na Fianna Éireann'.

Chapter 5

212 James Doyle, BMH WS 127.

213 Holland, BMH WS 280.

214 Henry Murray, BMH WS 300.

215 Martin, BMH WS 591.

216 *Report of the Royal Commission on the rebellion*, pp. 10, 39, 55.

217 John O'Callaghan, 'The Limerick Volunteers and 1916' in Ruán O'Donnell (ed.), *The impact of the 1916 Rising: Among the nations* (Dublin, 2008), p.14.

218 Áine Ceannt, BMH WS 264.

219 Peadar Doyle, BMH WS 155.

220 Barton, *From behind a closed door*, p.243.

221 Annie Cooney, BMH WS 805.

222 Brady, 'Some recollections of 1916 leaders', pp. 19–20.

223 Colbert, BMH WS 856.

224 For text, see Snoddy lecture.

225 Kathleen Clarke [Helen Litton (ed.)], *Revolutionary woman: My fight for Ireland's freedom* (Dublin, 1991), p.68.

226 Áine Heron, BMH WS 293.

227 Daly, 'Con Colbert', pp. 72–3.

228 Gregory Murphy, BMH WS 150.

229 Holland, BMH WS 280.

230 Martin, BMH WS 591.

231 John Styles, BMH WS 175.

232 Holohan, BMH WS 328; Byrne, BMH WS 167.

233 Holland, BMH WS 280.

234 Young, BMH WS 531.

235 Con Colbert to Gretta Colbert, April 1916 (National Museum, HE EW 505). The Museum catalogue dates the letter 23 April, but it is very difficult to decipher.

236 Holland, BMH WS 280.

237 Cooney, BMH WS 805; Colbert, BMH WS 856; Byrne, BMH WS 167.

238 Byrne, BMH WS 167.

239 Byrne, BMH WS 167.

240 Young, BMH WS 531; Holland, BMH WS 280.

241 Brady, 'Some recollections of 1916 leaders', pp. 19–20.

242 Cooney, BMH WS 805.

243 Byrne, BMH WS 167.

244 Snoddy lecture.

245 Collins, *James Connolly*, pp. 277–8, outlines the positions.

246 Doyle, BMH WS 186.

247 Doyle, BMH WS 186.

248 For more on these debates, see McGarry, *The Rising*, pp. 120–1, 188; Charles Townshend, *Easter 1916: The Irish Rebellion* (London, 2005), pp. 344–55.

249 Holland, BMH WS 280.

250 Doyle, BMH WS 155.

251 Holland, BMH WS 280; Doyle, BMH WS 155; Rose McNamara, BMH WS 482.

252 James Kenny, BMH WS 174.

253 Doyle, BMH WS 155; O'Callaghan, *Revolutionary Limerick*, p.47.

254 Holland, BMH WS280.

255 Holland, BMH WS 280.

256 Cooney, BMH WS 805.

257 Young, BMH WS 531; Holland, BMH WS 280; Ruairí Henderson, BMH WS 1686.

258 For a full account of events at the South Dublin Union in particular, see Townshend, *Easter 1916*, pp. 172–5.

259 Doyle, BMH WS 155.

260 Seamus Murphy, BMH WS 1756.

261 Young, BMH WS 531.

262 Holland, BMH WS 280.

263 Thomas MacCarthy, BMH WS 307.

264 Patrick Egan, BMH WS 327.

265 MacCarthy, BMH WS 307; Cooney, BMH WS 805; O'Grady, BMH WS 282.

266 Holland, BMH WS 280.

267 Byrne, BMH WS 167.

268 Holland, BMH WS 280; Brady, 'Some recollections of 1916 leaders', pp. 19–20.

269 Doyle, BMH WS 168; Snoddy lecture.

270 Byrne, BMH WS 167.

271 Holland, BMH WS 280.

272 Seamus Kenny, BMH WS 158.

273 James Kavanagh, BMH WS 889.

274 Cooney, BMH WS 805.

275 Doyle, BMH WS 168.

276 Byrne, BMH WS 167.

277 Holland, BMH WS 280.

278 Holland, BMH WS 280.

279 Thomas Gay, BMH WS 780.

280 Daly, 'Con Colbert', p.73.

281 Holohan, BMH WS 328.

282 Joseph Reynolds, BMH WS 191.

283 Ceannt, BMH WS 264.

284 Byrne, BMH WS 167.

285 National Archives of England, War Office 71/352.

286 Laurence O'Brien, BMH WS 252.

287 Murray, BMH WS 300; Ó Sé, 'Na Fianna Éireann'.

288 McNamara, BMH WS 482.

289 Holland, BMH WS280.

290 White, *Dictionary of Irish biography*.

291 Holland, BMH WS 280.

292 Cooney, BMH WS 805.

293 Sheila Murphy described her time in Jameson's to Piaras F. MacLochlainn. See Piaras F. MacLochlainn, *Last words: Letters and statements of the leaders executed after the Rising at Easter 1916* (Dublin, 1990), p.150.

294 Bushell, MSP 34REF22326; Mollie O'Hanlon, MSP 34REF43514.

295 Holland, BMH WS 280.

296 Cooney, BMH WS 805.

297 Holland, BMH WS 280; Doyle, BMH WS 168; McNamara, BMH WS 482; Murray, BMH WS 300.

298 Byrne, BMH WS 167.

299 Cooney, BMH WS 805.

300 Margaret Kennedy, BMH WS 185.

301 Doyle, BMH WS 168.

302 Holland, BMH WS 280.

303 Murray, BMH WS 300.

304 Holland, BMH WS 280.

305 Holland, BMH WS 280.

306 Another Holland brother, Frank, was in the South Dublin Union.

307 Bob Holland statement (National Library of Ireland [NLI], Colonel Joseph Leonard Papers, Manuscript [Ms.] 33,700).

308 Doyle, BMH WS 186.

309 Holland, BMH WS 280; Holland statement (NLI, Colonel Joseph Leonard Papers, Ms. 33,700).

310 Young, BMH WS 531.

311 Ceannt, BMH WS 264.

312 Cooney. BMH WS 805.

313 Young, BMH WS 531; Ó Sé, 'Na Fianna Éireann'.

314 McNamara, BMH WS 482.

315 McNamara, BMH WS 482; Doyle, BMH WS 168; O'Neill, BMH WS 203; Holland, BMH WS 280.

316 Holland statement (NLI, Colonel Joseph Leonard Papers, Ms. 33,700).

317 Holland, BMH WS 280.

318 Holland, BMH WS 280.

319 McNamara, BMH WS 482; Holland, BMH WS 280.

320 Holland, BMH WS 280.

321 Holland, BMH WS 280.

322 McNamara, BMH WS 482.

323 Holland, BMH WS 280.

324 Barton, *From behind a closed door*, p.245.

325 McNamara, BMH WS 482.

326 Gay, BMH WS 780.

327 Murray, BMH WS 300.

328 Ceannt, BMH WS 264.

329 Cooney sisters, BMH WS 805.

330 Holland, BMH WS 280.

331 The two men gave several accounts of how the day unfolded. Their Witness Statements to the Bureau of Military History are drawn on here: Fr. Aloysius, BMH WS 200; Fr. Augustine, BMH WS 920.

332 Kennedy, BMH WS 185.

333 MacLochlainn, *Last words*, p.150.

334 Holland, BMH WS 280.

335 Holland, BMH WS 280.

336 Murray, BMH WS 300.

337 Cooney, BMH WS 805.

338 Murphy made this statement to Piaras F MacLochlainn. See MacLochlainn, *Last words*, pp. 145–6.

339 Gay, BMH WS 780.

340 George Nolan, BMH WS 596.

341 Holland, BMH WS 280.

342 O'Brien, BMH WS 252.

343 Holland, BMH WS 280.

344 Cooney, BMH WS 805.

345 McNamara, BMH WS 482.

346 Cooney, BMH WS 805.

347 Ceannt, BMH WS 264.

348 Kennedy, BMH WS 185.

349 McNamara, BMH WS 482.

350 Kennedy, BMH WS 185.

35 Byrne, BMH WS 167.

352 Holland, BMH WS 280.

353 Doyle, BMH WS 168; Holland, BMH WS 280; Ceannt, BMH WS 264; O'Brien, BMH WS 252.

354 McNamara, BMH WS 482.

355 Holland, BMH WS 280.

356 Seán Enright, *Easter Rising 1916: The trials* (Dublin, 2014), p.186.

357 Holland, BMH WS 280.

358 McGarry, *The Rising*, p.263.

359 O'Brien, BMH WS 252.

360 Murray, BMH WS 300.

Chapter 6

361 Lawless, BMH WS 1043.

362 Holland, BMH WS 280.

363 Byrne, BMH WS 167.

364 See Enright, *Easter Rising 1916*; Adrian Hardiman, '"Shot in cold blood": Military law and Irish perceptions in the suppression of the 1916 rebellion' in Gabriel Doherty and Dermot Keogh (eds), *1916: The long revolution* (Cork, 2007), pp. 225–49.

365 Enright, *Easter Rising 1916*, pp. 1–4, 43–5.

366 Collins, *James Connolly*, p.297.

367 Barton, *From behind a closed door*, pp. 28–35.

368 Hardiman, 'Shot in cold blood', p.229; Enright, *Easter Rising 1916*, p.29.

369 Barton, *From behind a closed door*, pp. 28–35; Enright, *Easter Rising 1916*, pp. 4, 46,

62–3; Collins, *James Connolly*, p.298.

370 Enright, *Easter Rising 1916*, p.30.

371 Barton, *From behind a closed door*, pp. 36–8.

372 McGarry, *The Rising*, p.270.

373 Brian Hughes, *Michael Mallin* (Dublin, 2012).

374 National Archives of England, War Office 71/352; Barton, *From behind a closed door*, pp. 36–8; Enright, *Easter Rising 1916*, pp. 23–4.

375 Enright, *Easter Rising 1916*, p.34.

376 Barton, *From behind a closed door*, pp. 36–8.

377 Gerard Doyle, BMH WS 1511.

378 Enright, *Easter Rising 1916*, pp. xii, 63–4.

379 National Archives of England, War Office 71/352.

380 Barton, *From behind a closed door*, p.247.

381 Holland, BMH WS 280; O'Neill, BMH WS 203.

382 National Archives of England, War Office 71/352.

383 Barton, *From behind a closed door*, p.247.

384 Liam Cosgrave, BMH WS 268, Appendix.

385 National Archives of England, War Office 71/352.

386 Townshend, *Easter 1916*, p.279.

387 Townshend, *Easter 1916*, p.283.

388 Barton, *From behind a closed door*, p.241.

389 Enright, *Easter Rising 1916*, pp. 71–2, 200–5.

390 The National Museum holds five of the eleven original letters: to Lila (HE EW 501); to Jim (HE EW 502); to Mack (HE EW 503); to Gretta (HE EW 504); and to the Dalys (HE EW 147). Colbert's letters to his aunt, Mary O'Donnell, and his cousin, Máire, are held in Kilmainham (7LR-1D41-15). The text of ten letters is published in MacLochlainn, *Last words*, pp. 146–50. The missing letter is that to Maggie Clarke, a copy of which appears in her brother Joseph's Military Service Pension File, MSP 24A1135.

391 Holland, BMH WS 280.

392 Ceannt, BMH WS 264.

393 Annie and Lily Cooney, BMH WS 805.

394 MacLochlainn, *Last words*, pp. 150–2.

395 Enright, *Easter Rising 1916*, pp. 37–8, 77–80, 239; Collins, *James Connolly*, p.307.

396 McNamara, BMH WS 482.

397 Enright, *Easter Rising 1916*, pp. 80–1.

398 National Archives of England, War Office 71/352.

399 Enright, *Easter Rising 1916*, p.81.

400 *Irish Times*, 18 January 2014.

401 MacLochlainn, *Last words*, pp. 152-3.

402 Barton, *From behind a closed door*, p. 247.

403 Milo McGarry, BMH WS 356.

404 Irish National Aid and Volunteer Dependants' Fund [INAVDF] Papers Report,
including financial statement, of the Executive of the Irish National Aid Association,
May 18 1916 – August 19 1916 (NLI, Ms. 24,375).

405 Executive minutes (NLI, INAVDF, Ms. 23,469); Clarke, *Revolutionary woman*, pp.
136–7.

406 Executive minutes (NLI, INAVDF, Ms. 23,469).

407 List of men executed with details of aid advanced to their dependants (NLI,
INAVDF, Ms. 24,360); Clarke, *Revolutionary woman*, p.125.

408 All relevant material is in MSP DP9900.

Chapter 7

409 This memorial has since disappeared.

410 *Irish Independent*, 2 May 1958; *Limerick Leader*, 5 May 1958.

Index

A

Aiken, Minister for Defence
 Frank, 220-2
Albert, Fr, 140
Aloysius, Fr, 181-2
American Relief Fund, 219
An Claidheamh Soluis, 81-2,
 84, 99
An Cumann Cosanta, 111
An Macaomh, 26
An Scoláire, 26
Ancient Order of Hibernians,
 The, 122-3
Armstrong, Major James A,
 198, 200-3
Army Pension Acts, 219-20
Ashe, Thomas, 203
Asquith, Prime Minister
 Herbert, 96, 199, 202
Aud, 136
Augusteijn, Joost, 43
Augustine, Fr, 181-2, 216-17

B

Baden-Powell, Robert, 69-70
Beaslai, Piaras, 101
Boland's Mills, 150
Bowen-Colthurst, Captain
 John, 197
Boy Scouts, The, 69-70
Brady, Seán, 78, 80, 139, 148,
 160
Breen, TD, Dan, 122, 220-1
British Army,
 Engagements with, 72, 166-
 9, 172, 175-8, 181-2
 Influence on the Volunteers,
 77, 94, 108, 120
 Recruitment in Ireland, 70,
 103, 110-11, 121, 123, 157,
 159
 see also Surrender
Brugha, Vice-Commandant
 Cathal, 154, 191
Bureau of Military History,
 25, 163
Bushell, Ellen Sarah, 46, 166
Butler, Mick, 171
Butler, Walter, 171

Byrne, Christy, 48, 109, 138,
 147-8, 161-2, 164, 167, 187,
 192-3, 210
Byrne, Tom, 140

C

Carey, Brother, 88
Casement, Roger, 28, 101, 121,
 195-6
Catholic Bulletin, 28
Ceannt, Áine, 137, 164, 174,
 180, 209, 211, 218
Ceannt, Commandant
 Éamonn, 101, 131, 135, 137,
 144, 150-1, 154-7, 160-1,
 165, 184-7, 190-1, 195, 198,
 200-1
Chamberlain, Inspector-
 General Colonel Sir Neville,
 83
Childers, Erskine, 114
Christian Brothers, 35, 39-40,
 176
Christian, William, 80
Clann na nGaedheal, 60
Clarke, Joseph, 36, 209
Clarke, Kathleen, 142, 218
Clarke, Liam, 119, 138
Clarke, Maggie, 36, 204, 209
Clarke, Tom, 21, 28-9, 67, 84,
 93, 101, 116, 120-1, 125,
 127-8, 131, 135, 143-4, 150,
 189, 195, 204
Colbert, Bridget, 32-3, 51, 53-
 4, 219, 222
Colbert, Catherine (Katty), 32,
 34-6, 50-1, 53, 129, 207
Colbert, Dan, 32-4, 38, 51
Colbert, Dr John, 37
Colbert, Elizabeth, (Lila), 29,
 31-2, 35-6, 37, 45, 51, 53, 70,
 77, 80, 139, 203, 205, 210-12,
 217, 219, 222-4
Colbert, Honora (Nora) née
 Mc Dermott, 31-3
Colbert, Jim, 32-3, 36, 50, 53,
 70, 129, 206
Colbert, Johane (Nan), 32-3,
 51-2, 205
Colbert, John, 21-3, 32-3,
 34, 38, 48, 50, 52-3, 55, 58,
 61, 80
Colbert, Margaret (Gretta), 32,
 36, 50, 53, 146, 207, 219
Colbert, Mary (Ciss), 32, 35,

 51, 53
Colbert, Mary née Condon, 31
Colbert, Michael (Mack), 32,
 36, 50, 53, 206, 219-22
Colbert, Michael William,
 31-2, 34
Colbert, Nora, 32, 36, 50,
 53, 206
Colbert, Norah, 33
Colbert, William Jr, 32-4
Colbert, William, 31-2
Coldrey, Barry, 39-40
Collins, Con, 120
Columba, Sr Mary, 223-4
Connolly, James, 104, 108, 131,
 144, 150, 161, 196, 198
Conscription, 103, 127, 134,
 189
Cooney, Annie, 138-9, 147-8,
 166-7, 174, 180, 183, 185-6,
 209-10
Cooney, Lily, 148, 209
Cosgrave, Quartermaster
 Phil, 191
Courts Martial, 21, 104, 164,
 188, 191-204, 214
Cumann na mBan, 138, 140,
 142, 150, 154, 165-6, 175,
 177
Cumann na nGaedheal, 67
Curragh Mutiny, 100

D

Daly, John, 107, 115-16, 121,
 127-8, 208
Daly, Kathleen, 143
Daly, Madge, 29, 37, 79, 116,
 122, 124, 128, 143, 163
Daly, Ned, 21, 29, 37, 84, 94,
 115, 117, 120, 128, 144, 150,
 195, 198, 202
Daly, Nora, 225
Danaher, Bride, 52
Danaher, Kevin, 129
Danaher, Tommie, 52
Danaher, William, 129
Dann, Alfred, 36
Dann, Emma, 36
de Valera, Éamon, 119, 150,
 203
Defence of the Realm Act
 (DORA), 102, 120, 193
Devine, Fr, 205
Dickson, Second Lieutenant
 AA, 214

Dore, Éamon, 94, 225-6, 228

Doyle, Quartermaster Peadar, 109, 154, 188

Doyle, Thomas, 167, 172

Dublin Metropolitan Police (DMP), 49, 191

Dublin Special Branch, 120

Dungannon Clubs, 67-8

E

Easter Rising, The, 109, 134-6, 140, 147-8, 150-2, 154-62, 165-6, 168-71, 175-80 *see also* Surrender, Courts Martial, Executions
Aftermath, 16, 28, 110, 152-3, 194
Planning of, 113-14, 127-9, 132-5, 137-8, 142-6

Education, 40-2, 71-2, 74 *see also* Christian Brothers

Egan, Patrick, 159

Emerald Square, 150, 154, 165, 175

Emmet Hall, 108, 137

Emmet, Robert, 89, 176

Evening Herald, 215

Execution, 194-7, 199, 218
of Colbert and his attitude towards it, 15, 20-1, 27, 37, 163-4, 189-90, 200-17, 228

F

F Company 4th Battalion Dublin Brigade, Irish Volunteers, 108-10, 112, 124, 137, 144-5, 147, 150-1, 154, 155, 158, 160-2, 165-8, 172-3, 188, 192, 201 see also Watkins' Brewery, Marrowbone Lane (Jameson's Distillery)

Fenians, 37-9, 42, 88, 94, 99, 137

Fighting Stories, 163

Fitzgibbon, Seán, 100-1

Fitzpatrick, David, 39

Four Courts, The, 150

Frew, Major DB, 200

G

G Men, 191-2, 199

Gaelic Athletic Association, 44, 102

Gaelic League, 44-6, 48, 51, 55-6, 74, 83, 89, 103, 148, 165, 230

Gay, Thomas, 163, 179, 185

Germany, 100, 114, 120-1, 132, 134, 136, 175-8, 197-8

Gibbs, Philip, 73

Gifford, Sydney, 90

GPO, 15, 140, 150, 161, 180

Gregan, Councillor, 90

H

Hamilton-Gordon, Lord Lieutenant Lord Aberdeen John, 57

Hart, Peter, 40

Hay, Mairne, 92, 113

Hayes, Jim, 52

Hayes, Mike, 52

Healy, Fr, 205

Heathcote, Major CH, 213

Heron, Áine, 142-3

Heuston, Seán, 21, 37, 70, 84, 92-3, 119-20, 127, 150, 195, 198, 202, 210, 212, 214-15

Hibernian Rifles, 150

Hobson, Bulmer, 67-8, 70, 75, 82, 93, 95, 99, 101, 108, 117, 120, 124-7, 132-3, 136, 230

Holland, Bob, 48, 75-7, 79, 117, 122, 144-6, 154-5, 157-8, 161, 163, 165, 167, 169-74, 177, 180, 182-3, 185, 187-9, 201, 204

Holland, Dan, 158

Holland, Walter, 171-2

Holohan, Gary, 25, 46, 48, 69, 80, 114, 124, 163-4

Home Rule, 17, 42-4, 96-100, 103-7, 229

House of Commons, 96, 100, 217

House of Lords, 96

Howth Gun-Running, 72, 100, 114-15, 144, 155, 169-70

I

Inspector General of the Royal Irish Constabulary, 99-100, 116

IRB, 58, 67, 84, 92, 95, 99, 112, 124-6
and the Rising, 127, 133-5, 144 *see also* Military Council, and the Volunteers

and the Volunteers, 95, 99, 101, 107-8, 122
Dublin Centres Board, 93, 144
John Mitchel Literary and Debating Society, 93, 125-6
Recruitment, 70, 91, 93-5, 113, 129
Military Council, 21, 131, 133-5, 144, 147, 151-3
Supreme Council, 93, 134

Irish Brigade, 121

Irish Citizen Army, 108, 126, 133, 150, 165

Irish Language, 36, 39, 45-9, 53-5, 68, 84, 88-9, *see also* Gaelic League

Irish National Aid and Volunteer Dependants' Fund, 218-19

Irish National Theatre Society (Abbey Theatre), 81

Irish Parlimentary Party, 43-4, 49, 55, 84, 96, 100, 103, 106, 218, 229

Irish Transport and General Workers Union, 90, 108

Irish Volunteer, 117, 120

J

Jacob's Factory, 150, 161, 164, 179, 181, 198, 201

James, Major WR, 200

Judge, Michael, 101

K

Kavanagh, Seamus, 85

Kennedy, Margaret, 187

Kennedy, Seán, 46

Kenny, Lieutenant James, 154

Kenny, Quartermaster Seamus, 162, 191

Kent, Thomas, 195

Kilmainham Gaol, 24, 187, 202, 209-10, 214

L

Larne Gunrunning, 100, 115

Lawless, Joseph, 24-5

Liberal Party, 55, 96, 98, 104

Liberty Hall, 90, 150

Limerick Leader, 120

Lloyd George, Chancellor for the Exchequer David, 27, 96

Lonergan, Michael, 82, 92-3, 99

Lowe, Brigadier-General William, 181-2

Lundon MP, William, 105-6

M

MacCaisin, Seamus, 82

MacCarthy, Captain Thomas, 159-60

MacCurtain, Tomás, 120

MacDermott, Lizzie, 33, 51

MacDiarmada, Seán, 28, 67, 84, 93, 101, 120, 125, 127-8, 131, 135, 142, 150, 189, 196

MacDonagh née Gifford, Muriel, 90

MacDonagh, Thomas, 28, 72, 90, 99-101, 118, 131, 144, 150, 161, 179, 181-3, 195, 201, 219

MacNeill, Eoin, 83, 99, 101, 103, 125, 134, 136-7, 147

MacNeill, Neil, 125

MacSwiney, Terence, 120

Madden, Michael, 23, 34, 37

Mallin, Commandant Michael, 108, 150, 196, 198, 202, 210, 212, 214-15

Marjoribanks, Ishbel Maria, 57-8

Markievicz, Countess Constance, 68-70, 75, 81-2, 90, 92, 115, 126-7, 150, 188, 198

Marrowbone Lane (Jameson's Distillery), 15, 140, 145, 156, 158, 160-87, 192, 198, 201, 204, 209

Martial Law, 102, 193

Martin, Eamon, 88, 90, 93-4, 99, 101, 125-7, 133, 144, 225

Maxwell, General Sir John, 193, 195, 199, 202, 203

McBride, Major John, 76, 144, 161, 190, 195, 201-2, 215

McDermott, Cornelius ,Connor', 31

McDermott, Sean, 191

McDonnell, May, 36

McDonnell, Nancy, 36

McGarry, Fearghal, 40, 45

McGarry, Seán, 93

McGowan, Josie, 169

McGrath, Joe, 185

McNamara, Rose, 175, 177-8, 186, 214

Mellows, Liam, 78, 86-7, 90, 93, 99, 119-20, 127

Mendicity Institution, 150

Molony, Helena, 113

Monteith, Captain Robert, 120-1

Moore, Colonel Maurice, 101

Murphy, Captain Seamus, 156, 161-7, 173, 178-80, 182-3, 186, 191-2, 227

Murphy, Sheila, 166, 174, 182, 209-10

Murray, Lieutenant Henry (Harry), 132, 163, 168, 180, 182-3, 190

Murtagh, Larry, 109

N

Na Fianna, 67-71, 73-6, 81-95, 112-13, 118, 121, 124-7, 150, 154, 165, 171, 174, 177 and Colbert, 46, 52, 54, 59, 68-9, 74-7, 81-2, 85-94, 114, 117-18, 126-7, 177, 193, 203 and the IRB, 70, 93-5, 107-8, 112, 125-6 and the Volunteers, 107, 113-15, 118, 120-1 An Céad Sluagh, 82, 89 Ard Choisde, 92, 125, 127 Ard Fheiseanna, 90, 92, 125-6 Headquarters Staff, 125, 127 Inchicore Company B, 117-18 Lord Edward Fitzgerald Sluagh (Limerick), 115-16 Militarisation, 87-8, 92, 113-14, 125-7 Scoil Éanna Sluagh, 91, 93 Sluagh Emmet, 89-90

National Association for the Prevention of Tuberculosis, 58

National University of Ireland, 49, 54

National Volunteer, The, 120

Nolan, George, 185

O

Ó Dubghaill, Seán, 83

Ó Riain, Pádraig, 81, 93-4, 99, 117-18, 127

O'Brennan, Lily, 180, 186, 209, 211

Ó Briain TD, Donnchadh, 222-3

O'Brien, Fr, 205

O'Brien, James (Bun), 36, 51, 53

O'Brien, Laurence, 165, 185

O'Connor, TP, 27, 55, 230

O'Donnell, Art, 92

O'Donnell, Máire, 208

O'Donnell, Mary, 207

O'Donnell, Roe, 60

O'Donnell, S, 50

O'Dwyer, Bishop, 84, 117

O'Hanlon, Mollie, 166

O'Hanrahan, Michael, 150, 195, 201-2

O'Keeffe, Josie, 169-70

O'Mahony, Fr, 140

O'Neil, Mick, 171

O'Neill, Edward, 109, 174, 201

O'Neill, Seán, 77

O'Neill, Sergeant Ned, 173

O'Shaughnessy, MP, PJ, 217

Orange Order, 98-9

P

Parliament Act, 97

Parnell, Charles Stewart, 43, 105

Partition, 17-18

Pearse, Patrick, 26-7, 55, 62, 71-3, 84, 89, 91-2, 99, 101, 107, 113, 120, 124, 131, 133, 135, 138, 144, 150, 153, 180, 192, 195, 197-8

Pearse, Willie, 72, 92, 195, 197, 202

Plunkett née Gifford, Grace, 90

Plunkett, Joseph, 72, 90, 99, 131, 135, 150, 189, 195

Poetry, 21, 47-8, 56-8, 61-3, 65-6, 89, 141-2, 149

Pounch, Seamus, 71, 80, 94

Power, Liam, 109

Prendergast, Seán, 28, 46, 76-7, 80

Proclamation of the Irish Republic, 16, 20, 28, 62, 131, 202, 217

Provisional Government, 181, 202

R

Redmond, John, 84, 96, 99-
101, 103-5, 112, 115
Religion, 24, 28-9, 42-3, 64-5,
75, 98, 142, 189, 205
Reynolds, Joseph, 164
Richmond Barracks, 110, 156,
160, 174, 186, 188, 191, 194,
196, 199, 202
Riordan, Mick, 172
Roe's Distillery, 156, 158-60,
165
Royal College of Surgeons, 150
Royal Commission on the
Rising, 127, 134
Royal Irish Constabulary
(RIC), 69, 71, 83, 87
Ryan, Desmond, 91, 107

S

Sapte, Lieutenant Colonel
Douglas, 199-200
Sherwood Foresters, 213
Scoil Éanna, 26, 71-4, 91, 93
Sinn Féin, 49, 83-4, 90, 99,
103, 120, 202-3, 220
Sinn Féin, 52, 54-5, 58, 81-4,
Smyth, Lucy, 139-41
Solemn League and Covenant,
97
South Dublin Union, 150-1,
155-9, 161, 166, 182, 187,
198, 201
South Staffordshires, 198
Stanley, Captain, 213, 214
St Patrick's Park, 182, 198, 200
St Stephen's Green, 150-1
Sunday Independent, 147
Surrender, 149, 163-4, 179-90,
198, 200, 203, 210

T

Tennant, Under Secretary of
State for War HJ, 217
Traynor, Minister for Defence
Oscar, 222-3

U

Ulster Volunteer Force, 98,
100, 103
Unionism, 17, 19, 96-9, 100,
104
United Irishmen, 43

V

Volunteers, The, 25, 93, 99-
102, 105, 107-8, 113
and Colbert, 77, 79, 99,
101, 107-9, 115, 117, 125,
128, 130, 138, 144, 146,
148 *see also* F Company, 4th
Battalion, Dublin Brigade
Executive, 99, 121
Irish (Sinn Féin) Volunteers,
83-4, 103, 111-12, 114-15
117, 119-24, 127, 132-7, 144,
147-8, 150, 153-4, 157, 169,
188, 169, 188, 200, 203
4th Battalion, Dublin
Brigade, 191
A Company, 132, 162-3, 192
C Company, 158-60, 165
E Company, 192 *see also*
F Company 4th Battalion,
Dublin Brigade
1st Battalion, 150
2nd Battalion, 118, 150
3rd Battalion, 118, 150
Dublin City and County
Board, 119
Executive, 99, 121
National Volunteers
(Redmondite), 103-4, 109-
10, 123, 144
Provisional Committee, 99-
101, 124
Split, 83, 103, 109, 112, 117
War of Independance, 32, 34,
92, 102, 184
Ward, Patrick, 94
Watkins' Brewery, 15, 145,
155-8, 160-2, 166, 174
Wellington Barracks, 145, 155
Whitsunday Manoeuvres 1915,
120-4
Wimborne, Lord Lieutenant
and Governor General
Baron, 193
Wolfe Tone, Theobald, 43
Women's National Health
Association, 58
World War I, 18, 72-3, 98, 102-
5, 110-11, 133, 143, 180, 194
see also Conscription
Woulfe, Dick, 34, 36, 207
Woulfe, Maurice, 34,
Wylie, Lieutenant William
G, 196

Y

Young, Tom, 109, 145, 154-5,
157, 173-5